INDIVIDUALIZED REMEDIAL READING TECHNIQUES FOR THE CLASSROOM

P9-CFX-014

by Deloise E. Kochevar

Here is an indispensable guide for teaching remedial reading in the classroom without the aid of a special instructor or special facilities. In this volume, the elementary teacher will discover new, practical and highly effective methods for teaching remedial reading in either the traditional or the open type of classroom. Each of the methods, techniques and procedures described here have been tested in an actual setting and have produced exceptional results. Designed to take the burden of planning and evaluating such a program from the shoulders of the already busy teacher, these methods can be put to use in the classroom immediately.

PARTIAL OUTLINE OF CONTENTS

1. Developing a Strong Remedial Reading Foundation.
2. Spotting the Disabled Readers—Understanding the Reasons for Reading Problems.
3. Phonics—A Sound Beginning for Remediation.
4. Oral and Audial Training on an Individual Basis.
5. Perception—The Unknown Quantity, and How to Measure It in Reading.
6. Dyslexia—What Is It, How to Spot It and What Remedial Action You Can Take.
7. Individual Tests and Testing Techniques That Bring Effective Remediation in Reading.
8. Individualized Reading Instruction to Fit Specific Needs.
9. Coordinating Your Remedial Reading Program with Other Subject Areas.
10. Tested Games and Activities that Increase Individual Reading Skills.
11. Techniques and Teaching Methods Uncovered by Recent Research and Development.
12. Evaluation and Setting Goals for Remedial Reading.

ABOUT THE AUTHOR

DELOISE E. KOCHEVAR is currently a second grade teacher in the Chadbourne Elementary School in Fremont, California. She has taught grades one through eight for more than thirteen years, and has conducted workshops and graduate level seminars in reading, language arts and social studies. She has had extensive experience in the area of remedial reading, and has credentials as a reading specialist and a private consultant on reading disabilities. She completed her M.A. in Elementary Education at California State University at San Jose.

She has written several articles for professional teachers' magazines, including *Instructor*, primarily in the field of reading and language arts. She helped author the Fremont Unified School District reading guide and the new social studies guide. Mrs. Kochevar is a member of the California Teacher's Association, the National Education Association, and the California Association for Neurologically Handicapped Children.

4

0-13-457192-4

Individualized
Remedial Reading Techniques
for the Classroom Teacher

Individualized
Remedial Reading Techniques
for the Classroom Teacher

Deloise E. Kochevar

Parker Publishing Company, Inc.
West Nyack, New York

Library of Congress Cataloging in Publication Data

Kochevar, Deloise E
    Individualized remedial reading techniques for the
classroom teacher.

    Bibliography: p.
    Includes index.
    1. Reading--Remedial teaching. 2. Individualized
reading instruction. I. Title.
LB1050.5.K575   372.4'3   75-15842
ISBN 0-13-457192-4

- Tested games and activities that increase individual reading skills.

- Individual tests and testing techniques that speed the progress of remediation.

- The latest data on perceptual disabilities, with remediation techniques for these types of disabilities.

- The latest information on "motor-control" activities that speed remediation progress.

- Suggestions on how to record students' progress, how to control and how to evaluate your program.

Emphasis throughout this book is on remedial reading programs that can be carried out in the classroom—whether it be the traditional or "open" type of classroom. And while these programs should produce excellent results, they will not interfere with the ongoing educational progress of the rest of your students.

How This Handbook Will
Help You Teach Remedial Reading

While this is the age of specialization, and some school districts employ reading specialists, others lack sufficient funds to institute a full-scale remedial reading program. Most federal- and state-funded remedial programs require minimum standards on staffing or pupil-teacher ratios. This often makes such a program prohibitively expensive, especially for small districts. For this reason, remediation frequently becomes the responsibility of the classroom teacher.

This book offers practical help in diagnosis and remediation—especially for the classroom situation. It provides suggestions and techniques which you can use either with small groups or with individuals, and they can be tailored to fit the needs of students *and* the time-scheduling problems of the teacher.

Advantages of a Classroom Remediation Program

There are many advantages in establishing a classroom remediation program. Here are some examples of ways in which this book will help you:

(1) You will be able to spot reading weakness in content areas as well as in the reading curriculum.

(2) You can work with an individual child, or with small groups that have the same kind of reading weakness, while other children are busy with group tasks.

(3) Along this line, you can teach to improve each child's weakness, and further individualize instruction.

(4) There is no stigma attached as the child is not singled out for removal from the classroom to a special teacher.

(5) The teacher can gear the materials in other curriculum content areas to the needs of her students, thus providing special materials that they can read.

(6) Rapport with each student can be maintained, and through this, the teacher has a better relationship to improve the child's reading.

(7) The teacher has a more complete knowledge of the child than an outside reading specialist and this gives an added advantage. By knowing the child's interests, these can be utilized to stimulate further reading.

(8) By working within the classroom the students can read together in pairs, or other students can help with the drill work.

Format of the Handbook

The book is organized into three main parts. The first area, composed of the first four chapters, is devoted to spotting weaknesses, the general causes of reading difficulties, and discusses the importance of phonics instruction and when phonics instruction should begin.

The second part will help you identify remedial students according to their needs, and includes a special section on perceptually disabled and dyslexic students in the classroom. To enable the teacher to identify the remedial students in the classroom, the chapter on tests and testing techniques (including instructions for teacher-made tests) has been placed here.

The last section suggests ways in which the teacher can correlate the program in other curriculum areas. Emphasis is placed on individualizing the instructional program within the classroom. With this thought in mind, I have included examples of simple, inexpensive materials the classroom teacher can make or obtain that will help to further improve the program. There are word games and puzzles, some teacher-made and others which can be purchased at very little cost. In this section you will find a short chapter on some current, revealing trends in reading and guidelines to teacher evaluation of the program. At the end of Chapter 12, I have included a list of high interest-low vocabulary reading series which are very useful on an individual or small group basis.

Most teachers like a bibliography that includes some of the current books on reading and the different reading theories. I have listed some of the books which I have found helpful in my own reading program.

This book will provide competent, calculated answers to three key questions:

1. What is reading failure?
2. How do we identify a child with a reading disability?
3. Once recognized, how do we treat the symptoms?

Reading disability definitely *has* symptoms, and once these are diagnosed, the teacher can begin remedial instruction to alleviate the symptoms. (Reading disability is the one area in which the instructor can safely use the symptom to cure the disease!)

Deloise E. Kochevar

ACKNOWLEDGEMENTS

The author sincerely appreciates the help and advice from the following personnel and staff of Fremont Unified School District: William Bolt, Superintendent; Olga Madison and Berdie Cannon, Food Services; Dolores Rose and Jane Trout, Instructional Materials Center; Harold Clayson, Principal; Marian Seitzer, School Nurse; Jean Combis, School Psychologist; and the members of the Research and Development department. Grateful acknowledgement is also given to Wanda Laudenslager, Director, Speech, hearing and language department, Newark Unified School District. I am indebted to many teaching colleagues who offered suggestions and advice to help in my writing.

D.E.K.

Contents

Individualized
Remedial Reading Techniques
for the Classroom Teacher

1

Developing a Strong Remedial Reading Foundation

How and Where Do We Begin?

The field of diagnosis and remediation of reading difficulty is so broad that whole volumes are written on the subject. The purpose of this book is to give specific techniques which are applicable to the classroom and can be carried out with a minimum of extra preparation time and maximum efficiency. These can also be carried into related curriculum areas for reinforcement and skills mastery in the target areas.

This chapter will cover identification of students who might be suffering a reading handicap. Methods given are just a quick overview which will be expanded in Chapter 2. Listed will be quick testing techniques which can be utilized to establish proof of reading disability. (Using a written or printed test is valuable as a reference for record keeping or to pinpoint exactly which areas of reading need remediation for each student. Some children may be deficient in one area while others will need an entirely different kind of help.) Suggestions are then given for organizing a classroom program: (1) grouping for the needs of the students, and (2) materials (both teacher-made and commercial,) that can be utilized to aid in testing, record keeping, and setting up criteria for classification of a student needing remedial help. But first, remediation and individualization must be defined.

What Is Remediation?

To remediate is to make right, repair, or rectify. It is treatment which corrects. It is a means of stopping wrong habits or practices and of enforcing the right ones. Remediation requires evaluation of a student's attainment level and a teacher's subsequent effort to help the child toward more efficient learning. Success occurs in remediation when the teacher has changed the dynamics of the activity and redirected the attitude of the student from the negative to the positive.

The basic premise of remediation is taking a child at his present mastery level, and working from this point, helping him overcome weaknesses and attain proficiency at a higher step. The child needs to work from his present level through specific areas of remediation, developing wider ability and moving to a higher stage of attainment.

Individualization Defined

Carrying the aforementioned premise a step further, individualization is just what the term implies. It is taking the child at his present attainment level, and working with him on a one-to-one basis, fitting his remedial program to his personal needs. By using an individualized approach, rapport is quickly established, and the child feels the personal interest and concern of the teacher. Individual guidance and attention provide support for the child at a time when it is most needed, when he is feeling lack of success because of a lack of reading skills. A thwarted, frustrated child is an unhappy child. When a child is unhappy, he can't learn, thus his reading disability becomes a vicious circle. Our goal, by working with such a youngster on an individual basis, is to break this chain.

What Is a "Reluctant Reader"?

In this handbook, the term "reluctant reader" is defined as any student who has normal intelligence and probably can read, but will not. By definition, a "reluctant reader" is a child of normal intelligence who falls six months to one year below grade level in reading ability in the intermediate grades, and who falls at least six months below grade level in the primary grades. This child dislikes reading, but can't give a reason why. He might have had a problem earlier which caused an aversion to reading. A child who has moved from place to place frequently becomes a reluctant reader due to different school environments. He becomes confused, and doesn't understand the methods, goals, or customs. The constant moving about makes him feel insecure and inadequate. He is unable to cope with a constantly changing environment. It also poses problems for the teacher. It is difficult to plan a program for a student who may be with you only a short time. It is also the challenge inherent in individualization. Again, you take the child at his present attainment level, diagnose his needs, and work with him to help him improve.

What Is a "Retarded Reader"?

According to DeChant[1] a "retarded reader" is one who lacks over-all maturity in reading. The child is usually of average

---

[1]Emerald Dechant, *Diagnosis and Remediation of Reading Disability* (West Nyack, N.Y.: Parker Publishing Company, Inc., 1968), p. 9.

or above average intelligence (but could also be a slow learner). He may show blocks to learning, especially emotional or neurological blocks, which keep him from learning to read. Generally he has a low level of reading ability as compared to mental age, usually has normal intelligence, has had ample opportunity and tried, but still has not been able to learn to read. This child is usually more than one year below grade level in reading ability.

I recently discovered a child in first grade, Alan, whose behavior changed. He had been a happy child, and enjoyed reading games, and the listening activities connected with the phonics program. Then suddenly, temper tantrums, and pencil breaking appeared. He would sit and twist the pencil or crayon, but wouldn't write or color the exercises. By testing, it was discovered that the child had an auditory perception handicap. While others were able to listen to a set of directions, Alan could only hear *one* direction at a time. His brain could only accept one command to follow at a time, and thus he was becoming confused. By diagnosing the handicap, and by personalizing Alan's reading program, giving one step at a time, he was able to learn; his self-confidence was restored, and he began to move ahead in reading skills. By fitting his reading program to his needs (individualization), this child will enjoy a successful school career.

What Is a "Slow Learner"?

A "slow learner" is a child whose reading level is substantially below his mental age, but no specific problem exists. In other words, he is not as intelligent as the average child, but mentally is not so low as to be readily obvious. He learns only after a great deal of effort. Intellectually he is sub-normal and is a low achiever, scoring below the norm on a standard group I.Q. test. On the basis of other criteria he is not retarded to such a degree that he is a candidate for segregated instruction or for an Educable Mentally Retarded class. Probably he wasn't ready for initial reading experiences when they were first presented, and so fell further and further behind in his progress through the grades. Possibly there weren't enough readiness experiences and activities given this child. He needs more experience in reading and more instruction at his *present* level of ability. Implicit in this also is that a reading program be provided that motivates the child to learn. Further, he needs a much slower pace in keeping with his slower capacity to learn. By having a program fitted to his needs he will experience success, and feel secure and happy.

So we include in our categories all those students who are slow learners (normal I.Q.), reluctant readers, and retarded readers who fall within these academic standards. While this is an arbitrary position, it will be shown that techniques suggested will cover most classroom situations.

Levels of Learning

Any student's reading achievement can be classified as occurring on one of three different levels of learning: *mastery* level, *educational* level, or *frustration* level. Let me define:

Mastery level is that stage of learning at which the child knows the material. He can read it comfortably, understanding the concepts presented.

Educational level is the stage at which the student is introduced to new concepts and ideas which he learns easily and which provide stimulus to master the subject matter involved.

Frustration level is the stage at which the child is presented with new material, ideas, and concepts which are beyond his comprehension. In reading, this material is usually new vocabulary or word attack skills which are beyond the child's comprehension level. Since he doesn't understand, frustration results. Hence the term, frustration level.

Inasmuch as the classroom teacher already has the basic rapport, and also greater knowledge of the individual student's needs and weaknesses, the child would achieve better results in remediation than would occur in an outside-the-classroom situation. The child responds better within the familiar room environment. Except in cases of severe retardation, most authorities agree that children in the categories listed earlier in the chapter should receive their remedial instruction in their regular classroom with their regular teacher. Even those with overwhelming problems usually can be helped by use of a one-to-one situation. Only severely retarded readers who also are behavioral problems because of emotional disabilities need removal from their regular classroom situation for remedial help.

If the child falls *below* the criteria suggested, it is best to remove him from the classroom for special help. Children who fall more than one year below grade level usually have social and emotional problems connected with their reading disability which makes classroom remediation extremely troublesome for both the student and the teacher.

Seven Steps to Classroom Organization for Remediation

(1) The first step in setting up a classroom remediation center is to identify the students who have reading problems. Once the students have been identified, the program can be organized to fit individual needs.

Teacher observation is the quickest way to spot reading disability. Look around the classroom while the students are doing simple seat work. Who is squinting at the exercise before him? Who is curling or tearing the edge of the paper? Is someone daydreaming or drawing pictures on the edge of the worksheet? These general signs of restlessness may be clues to some kind of difficulty, usually related to reading. Watch for the child who will find any excuse to take him away from the task, such as sharpening his pencil, wanting to use the restroom or get a drink. Still other students might come to you for help, saying they don't understand. All these are possible *clues* to a reading problem.

You can check on vocabulary and comprehension with a quick oral reading survey. Have the child read instructions on a worksheet or the first few lines of a paragraph for you. If he miscalls words, substitutes other words, or can't sound out a word, then chances are he is experiencing reading difficulty. (If a student misses more than one word in 20 running words, the material is considered too difficult for him.)

You can also verify whether or not a child has a reading disability by looking at his cumulative records. Most cumulative record cards have places for posting reading scores, state testing scores, and other general information and will provide clues indicating past performance.

(2) After students with problems have been identified, reading tests should be given to diagnose the areas of weakness. There are many commercial tests available, or you can devise your own. Chapter 7 lists some of the best, most accurate tests published to date. If there are no commercial tests available, you can give the reading achievement test for the basal reading series the student used the preceding year. There is no harm in giving the test over again because in this case you are using the test as a *diagnostic* instrument only and looking for areas of weakness. Check to see in which categories the child's scores are lowest. These would be the areas of greatest need.

(3) When you have identified the types of weaknesses, you can begin to group your students and organize a plan of action. Choose one deficient area to work with at a time. Once the student shows progress in this area, you can move to another. If you try to correct problems in too many areas at once, the child becomes confused and unhappy. Remember, his learning capabilities (so far) have proved to be small and his attention span short. Lessons should be in keeping with this idea.

(4) Children should be grouped for remedial help, but

these learning groups should be small, not over two or three students, because this insures teacher control. With small groups, you can also better judge *who* is learning and who needs more individual help. Keep the lessons short, covering only one concept or practice area at a time. To reinforce these mini-lessons, plan varied seat work activities and games that can be completed easily by the students in the allotted time. Include in these activities simple paper and pencil games as well as drill, so that a variety of experiences are offered. (*Everything* about the learning pattern must be kept small except the teacher's enthusiasm, which must be great.)

When working with your remedial students, concentrate on only *one* area at a time. Sometimes when attempts are made to correct too many areas of weakness at once the student becomes confused. Too much material presented at too rapid a pace will result in confusion on the part of the learner, and he will be back at the "frustation level."

(5) To build confidence, at first choose materials that are at the student's mastery level. Then when the child feels more secure move into the educational level. In some cases, especially in the primary grades, you will need to go back to *pre*-reading skills and basic phonics instruction.

(6) Some form of record keeping, both for the remedial student and for yourself, is extremely important. A chart kept in colored inks or felt-tipped pens provides added stimulus to the child for improvement. Any form of record keeping that is convenient might be used. Experiment to find a way that suits you best. One way to keep a continuous record for the duration of your program is to put all pertinent information on file cards. These are handy and then can be used with the child in an inconspicuous manner, thus avoiding embarrassment. Permanent results should be recorded later on the cumulative record card.

(7) Once you have begun to chart your students' progress, review and evaluate to determine the *rate* of development for each child. No two children learn exactly alike or at the same rate. What might be a rapid rate for one will be too slow for another. Remember that even within a remedial group, learning rates will vary, so to coordinate your program for maximum efficiency, it is wise to check on pacing for each student. This is the purpose of individualization.

As the child gains mastery in one skill or content area, prepare for the next area of weakness to remediate. Choose your approach, materials, games, etc. so that your program never lags. One of the most difficult problems to combat is boredom stemming from inactivity. These children are apt to play anyway, and are used to sitting doing nothing out of sheer frustration. They need to be recalled to the tasks at hand more than other students. They are not self-directed, as they have little or no motivation due to their past failures. It is up to you as "motivator" to keep the students moving ahead in your program.

Reading research has proven that most remedial students never achieve nor maintain as much skill in reading as other students. These children will always need extra help and reinforcement, thus it is very important that the skills learned are *maintained.* You should frequently review the skills your students master during the program. Drill and repetition are a must so that these skills are not forgotten and lost again. Worksheets, games, and lessons should "spiral back" to reinforce the learnings. This spiraling back to maintain skills while moving forward to teach a new skill should be an integral part of your method.

Who Should Be Included in the Program?

The members of a remedial group will change from time to

time. If a student who normally progresses well in reading should suddenly develop a problem or have difficulty with a concept, you can move him into the remedial group for extra help and drill. When the difficulty is overcome, he should go back to his regular reading group. This can also be done for students who have a prolonged absence (one or two weeks or more) due to illness. When the lessons missed have been taught, this child also should return to this regular reading group. Use your remedial program not only to help the definitely diagnosed remedial student, but also to help other children who have difficulty with only one concept or skill. The remedial group is a good place to start a transfer student until he can be tested. You can observe and evaluate his reading skill better and faster in this smaller group.

Teacher evaluation is still the best standard for selection of remedial students. Your judgment as to who needs and can best profit from the program is still the best criteria.

Summary

Chapter 1 is primarily concerned with a general description for your basic plan of action. This chapter covers the first step, recognition of the problem—that is, the need for a remediation program for part of your students. Next, it covers classroom observation as a quick check for the students who are possible candidates for remediation.

Before the venture begins, there is a discussion of terms and how they are used in this book. In addition, criteria for placement in the remedial program are given. A seven-point organizational plan follows, so that you can begin classroom preparation and gather materials to get your program underway.

2

Spotting the Disabled Readers – Understanding the Reason for Reading Failures in Individual Students

This chapter covers the causes and symptoms of reading difficulties and includes suggestions on how to recognize and help the student with a reading problem. (There is a chart of common reading problems, with corrective methods, at the end of Chapter 3.)

Causes of Reading Disability:

There are seven basic causes of reading disability: (1) immaturity, (2) lack of readiness, (3) poor health, (4) poor vision or hearing, (5) bilingual environment, (6) perceptual handicap, and (7) low I.Q.

(1) *Immaturity:*

Here we have the child who started school before he was actually ready. In most cases, the youngster hasn't settled down to the routine of school work and would rather play than apply himself to the tasks at hand. He can only concentrate for very short periods, and wastes his time talking to neighbors, sharpening his pencil, or wanting to use the restroom. At primary level, he will be inclined to "tattle" on other students, blaming them for small incidents. Frequently, this type of child still resorts to tears when thwarted. He will do anything to get out of classwork.

Generally, the child is of normal I.Q. or higher, but is not ready to accept the responsibility of reading because he isn't yet interested. This type of child is seen most often in primary grades, but can be found in the upper grades as well. He is *not* hyperactive. Indeed, if anything, he moves at a little slower pace. His growth pattern may lag, thus the child may be small for his age. He is a good candidate for retention in first or second grade and should be given a chance to "grow up" (mature) a little, via retention, before he reaches the fifth or sixth grade, where he may be permanently lost if his immaturity persists.

Thus, if a child *does* need to be retained it's best to do so in primary grades, before he feels the frustration and inability to cope with the more advanced reading instruction and materials. There is little or no social or emotional damage in early retention, but a child retained at or above fourth grade is apt to suffer social stigma from his peers. Many times at the upper grades a student feels he has done the academic work once, and refuses to try the same grade level a second time.

For example, Richie L. was retained in fourth grade because he couldn't read or speak properly. He labored over each word while reading aloud, often hesitating and needing prompting. He read so slowly, and with such emphasis on sounding out words, that by the time he reached the period at the end of the sentence, he had forgotten what the sentence was all about. After several conferences, his parents and teacher decided to retain Richie and give him another chance. The principal arranged a transfer to another school within biking distance, so Richie could have a fresh start in new surroundings.

The youngster had always been popular in the neighborhood group, but now his former classmates teased him about being "held back." Richie became confused and angry, and fist fights broke out on the way to and from school. While the retention resulted in his academic work improving considerably, it was months before Richie adjusted to the move and made new friends.

Tommy L. was retained in second grade because of immaturity. Analysis of a perceptual examination indicated he also suffered from a visual perceptual handicap. Once his teacher was aware of the perceptual problem, special exercises and training periods were arranged, and Tommy was given special help. After having another chance at materials suited to his emotional and academic level, he became a happy, well-adjusted child, emerged from his shell, and became a playground leader. When in doubt, retain, *but do it early!*

(2) *Lack of Readiness:*

Lack of readiness means too few pre-reading experiences in kindergarten and grade one. Pre-reading skills and oral language development don't just "happen," but are carefully taught through well-organized plans. The tasks involved prepare the child for reading and are part of a highly-structured program. Readiness also applies to all phases of development: social and emotional growth, muscular coordination, and language abilities.

To be ready for formal reading instruction the child should have the following readiness skills:

A. Relationships: Associating pictured object with the spoken name for that object.

B. Visual discrimination: Four or five objects are pictured. The child matches two that are alike.

C. Auditory discrimination: The child sees a stimulus picture. He must mark each object in a series of drawings which begins with the same initial sound.

D. Word recognition: Three or four words are given on a printed page. The child must match picture with the correct word.

E. Sentence comprehension (spoken, usually involves child following directions given orally.)

F. Ability to count and write numbers.

G. Copying a model: The child duplicates one of a set of geometric figures or capital letters.

H. Drawing a human figure.

Danny was a child received as a transfer student. He was a small, handsome child who constantly brought gimmicks and gadgets to school. He would share these for a few minutes with friends, but would then accuse them of "taking" his things. He would wander around from desk to desk, annoying others while looking for his toys. No amount of persuasion would induce him to leave these items at home. He never attended to the work assignment unless prompted. At second grade, he still could not tell me the sounds of the consonant letters. He also had little or no basic sight vocabulary. Behavior patterns on the playground evidenced responses more like a beginning first grader than a second grader. He was obviously not ready for second grade, and needed to be retained because of this lack of readiness. Fortunately, Danny was put back in first grade at the proper social, emotional, and academic level. This occurred after conferencing with the parents, and re-testing by the school psychologist, who agreed with my diagnosis as to Danny's academic and maturity level.

There are many readiness tests available, and more information on them may be found in Chapter 7.

(3) *Poor Health:*

Students who fall prey to many colds or to a series of childhood diseases which cause prolonged absences will miss many pre-reading and language development experiences. Lack of these experiences, and later on, lack of basic instruction, may seriously retard development of reading skills. The beginning pre-reading experiences provide a solid foundation on which the teacher builds her program. These include not only the skills mentioned in the previous section, but also many language experience activities. For example, "Show and Tell" time encourages children to talk, and thus increases language facility and widens vocabulary. Also, it enhances social and emotional growth, as students learn to express themselves before a group of their peers. As an aside, the teacher also profits from "Show and Tell," for here is where she will discover shy, withdrawn children, and begin to work on social growth. If a child misses too many of these experiences, the teacher may not have sufficient time for individual help or tutoring to make up these losses.

It is sometimes difficult for the classroom teacher to explain to a parent the consequences of a child missing too many lessons in the pre-reading and beginning reading period. Most experts in the field of reading believe that poor attendance in primary grades seriously hampers a child's reading efforts, and that if it is impossible for the child to have "make-up" instruction to catch up with the class, it would be better to retain the child and give him a fresh start in pre-reading instruction and the basic reading skills.

Malnutrition causes many children to suffer educational handicaps as well as physical disabilities. Children who suffer from malnutrition and come to school hungry will not be able to attain as rapidly as students in good health. Children who appear sleepy, tire easily, suffer frequent colds, or generally appear listless may be suffering from malnutrition. They may be absent from school frequently and are usually poor readers. If a definite difference is noted after the child has eaten lunch, or after the mid-morning snack of milk and graham crackers (in primary grades), it is a good indicator that part of his educational handicap is due to inadequate diet. In such a case, the problem needs a two-pronged attack: that of diet and of remediation.

A home visit by the nurse is a possible solution to the diet problem. Many times, parents, particularly those of low income and transient labor groups, are not aware of the importance of proper nutrition.

Maria was referred to the school nurse because she was always rubbing her eyes. She had often complained of being cold and seldom played with the other children at recess, but sat huddled on the bench in front of the classroom. To escape the cold, she would beg the teacher to be allowed to stay in the classroom, to "help."

The school nurse arranged to make a home visit and asked Maria to interpret for her. With Maria's help, the nurse found that the family bought their groceries at a local store. She also discovered that the family "indulged" the children by buying pastries and carbonated beverages.

To many migrant families, food is a sign of prestige. Food dollars are spent on sweets and soft drinks to prove to others that they have money, too, to spend on these nice "extras." Such was the case of Maria, with too much of the family's food money being channeled in the wrong direction.

With the aid of the school nurse, Maria's mother was enrolled in an Adult Education class on nutrition and child care, and Maria was enrolled in the school free lunch program. Before the end of school Maria's over-all listlessness disappeared; she no longer felt cold all the time, and her school work improved considerably.

Continued home visits by the nurse indicated that the whole family's eating habits were changing as a result of information and help obtained through the district Adult Education program.

Information provided by workshops or Adult Education

classes helps migrant families improve their dietary habits. Classes conducted within our district use school facilities and school personnel; nurses, school lunch services administrators, dietitians, and cooks. These people provide valuable information and help in planning and conducting our nutrition education program.

Most health and science texts contain units on nutrition which can be utilized to teach students better dietary habits, and you can provide experiences and information as part of your classroom projects so that these children learn for themselves about diet. Since most of their parents leave for work before these youngsters are up, the children have to prepare their own breakfast. With a little information and some examples, these students might be able to provide better meals for themselves. Perhaps as a classroom project the class could plan and prepare breakfast together in the school cafeteria.

(4) *Poor Vision or Hearing:*

If a child has difficulty seeing the printed page or lessons on the chalkboard, then it follows that his skill in reading will be impaired. If the child squints, or says, "I can't see the board," he should be given a vision screening test. Most schools test certain grade levels annually, so that students get a vision check at one time or another in their school careers. For example, in our school district students are tested at first and fourth grades. However, the school nurse tests students at other grade levels as needed when a visual problem is suspected.

I must point out that most school-administered vision screenings are inadequate, as there are some vision problems, such as "lazy eye" (amblyopia), or farsightedness, that cannot be detected by most school equipment. *Every* child should have an eye examination by a medical professional before reaching second grade.

Equally serious are signs of hearing loss. If a child turns his head, seeming to favor one ear over the other, or frowns when listening, chances are he is having difficulty hearing. Another clue is frequent nasal drainage. If a child seems to have a cold most of the time, chances are he might also be subject to ear infections, which might affect hearing, either temporarily or permanently. If a hearing loss is suspected, it is advisable to have the school nurse or speech therapist give a hearing test. Also a quick "whisper test" technique which can be administered in the classroom is given in Chapter 7.

(5) *Bilingual Environment:*

Many students from bilingual families or foreign-born parents don't hear enough spoken English at home to build adequate language experiences. Children of families that move frequently and who don't have reading materials in their homes may also suffer reading difficulty. If reading isn't stressed at home, and if the adults themselves do little or no reading, the children then have no opportunity or incentive.

Many children from bilingual homes are ashamed of their background and embarrassed when their parents can't speak English. One solution is to *involve* the parents in school activities, and have them invited to help in school libraries and as aides in the classroom.

In our school district social studies program, we stress integration of all ethnic groups into our environment. Cultural contributions from people of foreign extraction are discussed, and children of different heritages are encouraged to share customs and experiences. Foods native to other countries that have become a part of the standard American diet (tacos from Mexico, matzos from Israel, and Baklava' from Greece) are prepared by mothers and brought in to be tasted and shared by the entire class. As children share these experiences with others, they develop pride in their cultural backgrounds, and through this generate better feelings about themselves.

Practice in reading is basic to learning, and without practice, a child will not progress quickly. Family attitudes and values toward education, particularly reading, can affect a child's behavior in this area. If his parents don't feel reading is important, or if they don't have time to listen to the child and help him, reading skills may be retarded.

Adult education classes are one answer to the problem. The parents should be encouraged to enroll in "English as a Second Language" courses. Library books written in Spanish and French should be available in libraries in elementary schools and children encouraged to take them home for their parents to read aloud. In districts which have a Spanish segment, notices of school activities should be printed in both English and Spanish, so that parents can be aware of what is happening in the schools. These people need to know that you are interested in them, and that their children's progress is important to you.

(6) *Perceptual Handicap:*

According to gestalt psychology, perception is the thing we *see* and how we interpret it. The parts of the image are classed as "figure" and "ground." The *figure* is the thing we perceive, and the *ground* is the background against which the figure appears. A student must be able to see this as an integrated relationship, that is, the parts to the whole. He must perceive the entities (pictures, letters, or words) as separate from the background in which they appear. When a student suffers from a perceptual handicap, the figure-ground percept is distorted. The message reaching the brain has been garbled, or short-circuited, if you will. What appears on the printed page has little or no meaning because of this disability.

According to Dr. Marianne Frostig, "Visual-motor coordination is the ability to coordinate vision with the movements of the body or with movements of a part or parts of the body. Whenever a sighted person reaches for something, his hands are guided by his vision. Whenever he runs, jumps, kicks a ball or steps over an obstacle, he directs the movements of his feet. In such everyday activities as getting dressed, making a bed, carrying a tray, entering a car, or sitting down at the table, the eyes and the whole body work together. The smooth accomplishment of nearly every action depends upon adequate eye-motor coordination."[1]

A child with a perceptual handicap has difficulty with many motor control activities. When checking for perceptual difficulty look for these symptoms: poor handwriting skills (letters may be large and ill-formed and will not "sit" on the line properly); poor drawing, cutting, and pasting; inadequate ability to sequence, both in spelling and reading. This child may appear clumsy in playground activities and generally will have a very poor self concept. Usually in primary grades, he still confuses left and right, and may have difficulty distinguishing different parts of his body. He may not perceive how he controls body movements.

This child usually makes letter reversals, and will write numbers backwards, such as "b" for "d," "p" for "q," etc. These reversals will appear consistently in the child's written work. He will reverse "s," and numbers like "5," "9," and "2," and often writes his letters moving in the wrong direction, forming them from right to left rather than from left to right, and from bottom to top rather than top to bottom.

This perceptual handicap may also influence the forgetting curve, as the child will have very poor visual memory, and can't recall words. This is due to an impairment which affects the way he sees and interprets configuration. It is more commonly termed *dyslexia*. (See Chapter 6.)

Perceptual handicaps can usually be corrected or reduced to a tolerable level. Success in correction depends on early detection and prompt therapy, which consists of "patterning" exercises and sets of coordinated muscular activities. Activities which are helpful are stringing beads, working with simple jigsaw puzzles, fitting nuts and bolts into correct openings, etc. Physical activities, which can be utilized in your physical education program are walking a balance beam, using a balance board, and jumping games using old automobile tires. A more complete list of games and exercises is given in Chapter 10.

---

[1]Marianne Frostig and David Horne, *The Frostig Program for the Development of Visual Perception* (Chicago: Follett Publishing Co., 1964), p. 16.

(7) *Low I.Q.:*

The child in this category generally works slower than other children. His motor and physical functions are good, he is usually in good health, and his size to age ratio is normal. However, his Mental Age will fall below Chronological Age to such an extent that he will score ten to 20 points lower on I.Q. tests—which will not be low enough to qualify him for the mentally retarded program. His academic progress will be six months to one year behind students in the normal range. Learning can be especially difficult for him.

This type of child will need more and longer experiences at pre-reading level, and a much slower pace in basic phonics instruction. It will take him much longer to master the pre-primer and primer levels and the basic sight word list.

Johnson[2] says the normal child is ready to move from pre-reading skills and the chart stage at C.A. six plus years, after about six to ten weeks of instruction, while those with lower I.Q. will not be ready for beginning reading until they have completed ten to 15 weeks of instruction. This retarded child's chronological age may be as much as seven years.

Many times a low I.Q. child will also have other physical impairments, such as vision or hearing problems. These factors must be considered when organizing a reading program and setting up a classroom environment, and must also be considered when individualizing for instruction. A low I.Q. child needs a slower pace, and experiences that maintain interest while reducing failure. Patience is the key to success, not only for the teacher, but for the student.

The Failure Syndrome—How to Spot Weaknesses

Children who fail often in their attempts at learning will refuse to try any longer. This is the "failure syndrome." It is the tendency to withdraw from any challenging situation if failure

---

[2]G. Orville Johnson, *Education for the Slow Learners* (Englewood Cliffs, N.J.: Prentice-Hall, Inc., 1963).

is probable. A child will use this mechanism against defeat and create for himself a smoke screen to cover his feelings of inadequacy. His attitude is, "If I'm going to fail, why try?" This refusal to try engenders in his classroom teacher a feeling of hopelessness and despair.

How do we recognize and help the child with the "failure syndrome" within a classroom of 30 other children? How can we identify the student who is experiencing frustration and defeat? He will tell us by his actions.

Watch for signs of difficulty during the library period. If a child shows little interest in books and becomes quickly bored with recreational books, he is probably a poor reader. He will wander around, picking up this book and that one—and all too often choose a book beyond his reading level. He will attempt to prove to himself and to others via this "hard" book that he is able to read. For a quick verification of book level, the teacher can turn to a page at random and have the student read it aloud to her. If the child misses more than one word in 20 consecutive words, the material is too difficult for him.

Watch for the child who is too quiet, particularly among the girls. It is very easy to overlook this child, especially if she is well-behaved and is not a discipline problem. Since she is but one of many children in the class, each needing instruction, discipline, and guidance, it is very easy to miss *one* child who has a reading problem, but is covering up with good behavior.

Be suspect of the good talker who reads poorly, writes poorly, but is seemingly very bright and full of information. This child is a good listener and picks up ideas fast, but has missed some basics somewhere.

The clown, "wiseacre," or showoff also might be experiencing difficulty. Many times, children with behavior problems are the disabled readers. Since they cannot win your approval, they must gain your attention, and the only way is through these behavioral symptoms.

Most poor readers are also poor spellers and consistently low grades on spelling papers, especially on a spelling dictation test, are good indicators of poor reading ability. If the child can't sound out words or divide them into syllables as aids in remembering how to spell them, he is a poor reader.

If you suspect that a child has a reading difficulty, have him read a short selection. Make out a list of questions before the child reads the given selection. By asking the student these questions, you can determine whether the child understands what he reads. If he stumbles over words, hesitates, repeats words or phrases, miscalls words, omits beginning or ending syllables, makes word or letter reversals, then he is experiencing reading difficulty.

Peer values develop very early, sometimes in first or second grade. Children don't want others to know they don't understand, therefore they become adept at hiding their disability. The teacher must be constantly alert to such a situation developing in her classroom. Watch for the furtive child, the ball of paper hidden in the jacket pocket, the secretive hand held over the book. This child is hiding!

Even the youngest students, those in first or second grade, know when they aren't performing as well as their classmates. Many times they are unable or afraid to express their lack of understanding to their teacher. *This* is when reading failure develops. The teacher must watch for this unease in her students, and then diagnose and correct the disability before moving on to more difficult concepts.

The best way to attack the problem is to try to reduce the student's feeling of inadequacy. By diagnosing the difficulty and working from the weak area, you can correct the disability and at the same time work to improve the child's self concept. He must be helped to develop confidence and pride. If he believes he can do something, he *will* do it.

For example, Jimmy L., a student with a small reading disability, suddenly developed poor work habits. The quality of his work dropped and the amount of written work turned in decreased sharply. He began to hide behind his book, propping it up on his desk. Jimmy made no effort to write, except when the instructor stood directly behind him or worked with him.

By careful questioning, it was found that Jimmy felt

unsure of himself. He felt "dumb." This information was obtained during a private session held after school, where he revealed that another classmate was teasing him, telling him he was dumb and stupid.

Remember, if you're told anything long enough, you may begin to believe it, and this was happening to Jimmy, badly damaging his ego and self concept. By getting at the root of the problem, and also working with the other youngster to see why he had to build his *own* ego at another's expense, both problems could be solved. The teacher could work on Jimmy's problems and feelings about himself, and also help the other youngster toward greater compassion and empathy for others.

Soon both youngsters improved, Jimmy in his reading disability and the other child in citizenship, and both became happier children.

Children with poor feelings of self-worth must be told over and over that they *are* important and that they *can* learn to read. Children with feelings of inadequacy or behavioral problems must be shown that there are *other* ways to gain attention through better social and emotional behavior because *they* have problems, too.

We are what we learn to be, and until late in maturity, we are malleable. A child is the most flexible, moldable creature imaginable and is easily damaged by lack of love and by criticism. A child needs to be taught that he is *someone.* You have this child six hours a day. Make the most of it!

3

Phonics, a Sound Beginning
for Remediation

The average child enters school with a speaking vocabulary of over 2,000 words, and a listening vocabulary of over 10,000 words. His period of greatest vocabulary growth will occur between the ages of two and eight years.

Pre-reading skills depend on visual, oral, and auditory discrimination. Phonics readiness like reading readiness, doesn't just happen, but is carefully taught. Training in these aspects is begun in kindergarten and continues on up through *all grade* levels to sixth grade.

Some children have a good "ear" for sound and are able to quickly learn the fine distinctions between the sounds they hear, but others are not able to make this distinction, and must be taught to listen for the different sounds and analyze how they are made. Children with problems in sound discrimination need to be taught to connect letter names to letter sounds, and must learn to identify the separate sounds in spoken words. They must recognize that many of the consonants and all of the vowels have at least two sounds. How do we figure out which sound to use where? How do we "decode" from symbol to sound? I will try to answer these questions in this chapter.

Sight vs. Sound, the Age-Old Controversy

For almost 200 years there was heated argument among educators as to the best method of teaching reading. Proponents of the "look-say," or word method felt the child should see the whole word and a picture of it. Then he would be able to connect the thought (or word configuration) with the visual cue (object), so that the word would appear in context.

Advocates of phonics believed that the sounds the letters made were the key to reading. If a child could identify the sounds, then he would be able to apply phonics principles to analyze known words.

Today most experts agree that teaching of reading is a blending of the two techniques, and that proper readiness involves the integration of both areas.

We now use four basic steps in phonics development: (1) visual discrimination, (2) auditory discrimination, (3) sound blending and (4) context clues.

Visual Discrimination. Building visual discrimination is an integral part of phonics! Readiness for phonics may begin simultaneously with readiness for reading. However, children need a basic sight vocabulary of known words to see the letters as the teacher presents her phonics lesson. This skill is introduced and extended through visual discrimination techniques.

If your remedial student is poor at visual discrimination, the logical steps for remediation would be (a) presenting pictures of objects mounted on cards; (b) showing the pictured object with the word printed next to it; and (c) presenting the word alone, with the picture on the back of the card. Thus the child moves from the concrete to the abstract symbol.

Later, simple sentences can be used to show the word in

context. Many of the Dolch games (published by Garrard Press) reinforce this principle, and the Dolch Basic Sight Word list is most helpful in building a basic sight vocabulary. Another list which is valuable in building sight vocabulary is the one compiled by Dr. Botel.[1]

Visual readiness is developed through the use of pictures, charts, scatwork activities and what I term *sight-sound synthesis*. This is done by using a visual cue (holding up a picture or object) and at the same time speaking the word slowly, so that the student hears *all* the sounds. The components of the word are not broken apart, but presented as one whole unit, so that the student can relate the parts as an analogous whole.

When a person is reading, each fixation of the eye will perceive only part of the letters in a word or phrase. An average reader in primary grades makes eight to 12 fixations per line, while in upper grades an average student makes only three or four fixations. As a student gains experience, the fixations become fewer and fewer. Thus, he "fills in" the material. He takes in a wider area on the printed page. He doesn't actually "see" the material between fixations but perceives it as a meaningful idea.

This skill develops during the learning process. When a student cannot fill in the missing parts in a drawing, or cannot pick out a form embedded in a larger picture, he is suffering from a visual closure deficit. (See Chapter 6.)

Remedial exercises must be built around experiences which help him organize and integrate the visual field in order to build a recognizable visual percept (idea). These include such activities as simple working with jigsaw puzzles, anagrams, dominoes, and playing card games which require rapid recognition of pictures. Complete the picture activities, in which the student is given a drawing with some lines or parts missing, and he fills in the missing parts, are also helpful.

There are many activities and games the teacher can use to remediate deficits in sight-sound synthesis. Workbook activities

---

[1]Morton Botel, *Botel Predicting Readability Levels* (Chicago: Follett Publishing Company, 1962).

which have the child look for similarities or differences in picture objects are very useful.

For example, a page may have a series of simple pictured objects with one object "framed" on the left. The child looks across the line, finds all of the objects like the one in the frame or box, and marks them. Later on, you can use pages where the child identifies all objects having the same initial sound as the framed object. In my own classroom, at primary level, I have students color the objects as a visual-perceptual exercise to develop hand-eye coordination.

Later the child is given a page on which a picture appears, as does the outline of the letter for the beginning sound. The child colors the picture, traces over the letter, and then practices writing the letter for himself on the worksheet, following the model. This provides positive reinforcement of the sound-symbol relationship.

Auditory Discrimination. Learning to *listen* is crucial to phonics readiness. Remedial students, especially those in primary grades, need a variety of listening experiences, and these, utilizing the vocabulary and prior training, are extended and reinforced through classroom activities. Clapping games in which students count the claps can be used. Singing games and nursery rhymes help children learn to discriminate between pitch and intensity, (high-low, loud-soft, near-far away, and so on). Finger play, marching, and simple dances help students develop a sense of rhythm. Speech *does* have rhythm. We "speed up" our talk when something exciting is happening, and slow down our speech when discussing everyday activities.

As the child progresses beyond these beginning remedial activities, the teacher introduces beginning sounds in familiar words. The student learns to identify those that are alike, such as the "m" in *m*other, *M*ary, *m*ilk. The next step in remediation is listening for "how words sound alike on the end," such as "t" sound at the end of ha*t*, si*t*, pe*t*. Subsequently, the teacher can move to rhyming words, such as h*e*, m*e*, tr*ee*, s*ee*; or m*an*, c*an*, f*an*. It is very easy to reinforce this area using nursery rhymes and counting songs, and the children enjoy it.

With older students, the teacher can play "Detective." Example; Find the word that *doesn't* belong with the group:

Mother, Mike, Fred, Mary

The student should respond *Fred* doesn't belong, because it doesn't begin with "m" sound.

During these initial steps the child's full attention should be focused on the listening activities. While working on auditory perception, nothing should be presented visually on the chalkboard or through experience charts. This does not mean that visual and auditory discrimination cannot be taught at the same time, but I would suggest that you teach separate lessons, spaced a bit apart during the day. Later the two areas can be combined for sound blending lessons.

Sound blending (pronunciation). The term "sound blending" means running the sounds together in the natural pronunciation of the word. This smoothing out process is the next progression in teaching phonics. As the term implies, this is the step in which the child uses phonics cues and configuration to figure out pronunciation of new words in a sentence.

Many students get bogged down on sound blending. They are so busy sounding out the consonants at the beginning and breaking a word apart, that they lose the context of the sentence. If a child encounters two or three words like this in a page of reading, he becomes frustrated and reading becomes a bore. For this child there has been too much instruction in phonics and not enough on word synthesis (sound blending).

During oral reading, watch for the child who subvocalizes and sounds out each component; such as b-a-ll (ball), oo-n (oon)—ball-oon, (balloon).

The best way to overcome this type of difficulty is to have the child begin anew to examine the complete sentence for meaning. He must learn to grasp the context. Then, from the context, and applying his phonics knowledge of beginning and ending sounds, he can guess at the meaning of the unknown word. Instruct the child to check whether or not the word he guessed makes sense in the sentence.

Most children readily adapt this technique to fit their needs. Only in rare cases do we find students with difficulty in this area once the technique has been explained. If the difficulty persists with a student, then the reading material is too difficult.

If a child *does* have difficulty, go back and work on building a larger sight vocabulary, and on comprehension via context clues. The child needs more drill in getting the meaning from his reading. After he reads a passage, make sure he can rephrase it in his own words.

Context clues. A technical definition for "context clues" is integrating and applying visual and auditory techniques and sound blending so that the child can determine the meaning of a new word when it occurs in his reading. This is the understanding and comprehension state. It differs from sound blending in that sound blending actually is pronouncing the word, while context clues involves meaning of the whole sentence, and in some cases, the whole paragraph. Context clues is where the child finally knows what reading is all about. Phonics thus depends on context for effective functioning of word perception (analysis) in reading.

The use of this skill will vary with different students and also with the different types of material presented. Usually the student will look at the word as a whole, with the meaning of the sentence in mind. If he doesn't immediately recognize the word, he looks to the component at the beginning. If this doesn't divulge the word's identity, then he applies word analysis techniques, associating sounds with their letters. By blending the sounds, he tentatively identifies the word and checks it against context to see if it makes sense.

Structural analysis. Although this category is placed last, actual teaching of structural analysis begins in the reading readiness stage with the use of visual and auditory discrimination techniques.

The child's basic sight vocabulary is based on configuration; therefore, as students learn words from the sight vocabulary list, they are practicing beginning visual discrimination techniques which will help them in the later development of the structural analysis skills. The oral-auditory drills in rhyming words, beginning sounds, and so forth will also sharpen their abilities in this area. Rhyming games help students find like components in known words, and games and songs with like initial and final consonant sounds help. (As an example, think of the old nursery rhyme "Peter Piper picked a peck of pickled peppers.") During "Show and Tell" time, children can get practice using "s" forms on the ends of words, and on the "ing" ending. This is a definite skill which can be capitalized on at the readiness level. At the pre-primer and primer level children should be made aware of "s" and "ed" added to verb forms and of "s" added to nouns to make them plural.

By the time students reach primer and first reader level they are ready for the use of the apostrophe for possessive nouns and for compound words. This latter stage is very important, as this is the student's first introduction to putting familiar words together to make a new word; but even more important, it is the child's first experience at breaking words *apart,* beginning structural analysis technique.

This first stage, in which a child breaks a word into components, is a prime factor in learning to unlock new words. It is one of the simplest I know of, and it appeals to remedial students because they can see the logic in it. Words such as cowboy, postman, and milkman are already in their vocabulary. Prefixes and suffixes and looking for the base words are then introduced.

It must be stressed that these introductory lessons place emphasis on the introduction of structural analysis through oral-auditory experience. Most reading series do not introduce the written form until the first reader. Actual writing of these forms as structural analysis exercises doesn't occur in workbook or practice exercises until second reader level.

BASIC PHONICS CHART

Reading Level	Order of Presentation
Readiness	Auditory perception of sounds in the environment. Visual discrimination of letters, objects, pictures of forms in the classroom. Awareness of the term *rhyme* and rhyming endings. Awareness of initial position sounds of *b, c, d, f, h, l, m, r, s, t.* Awareness of structure of simple sentences, speech sounds, and patterns. Variations of pitch; high-low, loud-soft, near-far away, etc.
Pre-primer	Visual discrimination of capital and lower-case letters. Word forms for basic sight vocabulary (beginning configuration). Auditory discrimination of rhyming endings. Reinforcement of letters presented at readiness level. Add *p, w,* hard sound of *g, c* in initial position. Introduce *k, p, t* in final position. Introduce short vowel sounds, *a, e, i, o, u.*
Primer	Visual perception of like word forms and figures. Review and reinforce capital and lower-case letter discrimination. Auditory-visual perception of rhyming endings. Auditory-visual discrimination of all consonants but *k, v, y, z* in initial position. Auditory perception of *s, m, n* in final position. Auditory-visual perception of *k, p, t* in final position. Introduce digraphs *ch, th, wh* in initial position.
First Reader	Understanding of the word *rhyme.* Visual discrimination of *k, v, y, z* in initial position. Introduction of the digraph *sh.* Visual perception of *d, l, m, n, r, s* in final position. Review and reinforce previous consonant skills. Substitution of initial consonants, including blends *bl, br, dr, fl, fr, gr, pl, st, tr.* Auditory perception of short vowel sounds with consonant in initial position. Review and reinforcement of previous skills.
Second Reader	Introduce substitution drill for final consonant position plus awareness and use of term "consonant blend and consonant digraph." Introduce in initial position

Reading Level	Order of Presentation
	blends *cl, cr, pr, sh, sn, qu,* and the consonant sounds for soft *c* and *g.* Introduce in medial position blend *nk* first lesson that shows consonants can appear in different positions other than initial or final. Auditory-visual perception of *x, cks, ll, ss.* Rule final double consonants make only one sound. Auditory-visual perception of digraphs *ck, ng, th* (voiced and voiceless). Later in the year, auditory-visual perception of initial blends *gl, gr, sc, sp, sw, spr, squ, str, thr.* Review and reinforcement of previously-learned skills.
Third Reader	Review and reinforcement of previous skills. Introduce the term *phonogram* (letter or group of letters that make only one speech sound, usually with an adjacent consonant, such as the *ake* in make). Reinforce voiced and voiceless *th.* Auditory-visual perception of digraphs *ch, ph;* initial blends *sm, tw.* Use of *l, n, r* in final unstressed syllables, such as maker.

Figure 3-1

4

Mastering Oral and Auditory Training
on an Individual Basis

It has been my belief that *in the beginning stages of reading,* children do not need, *nor should they have,* phonics instruction. Emphasis should be placed on building a sight vocabulary based on known words pertinent to the child's own experience, plus the words of highest utility from the basic sight word list.

The beginning reader uses form and configuration to identify a word, and by seeing it over and over again will learn to recognize it on sight. In the beginning the child must concentrate on what the word, or a sentence, is telling him. *Phonics would direct him to letters and sounds before he has looked for the meaning of what he is reading, and thus would interfere with comprehension.*

Children's reading material in primary grades is determined by experience, words they know when they hear the words spoken.

51

Many sight words violate phonetic principles and can't be learned by any other method except by sight—and since these words are absolutely necessary for the child to function effectively in mastering reading, this sight vocabulary is taught in first grade at pre-primer and primer level.

If we have so great an emphasis on sight vocabulary building, then why is there a need for phonics?

As the child progresses through the grades, the vocabulary load increases at an overwhelming rate. There are just too many words for the child to memorize. For example, in the second grade the number of new words introduced more than doubles; and by the fourth year, the vocabulary load is five times greater than the first year!

To compound the problem, the child is being bombarded with new words, unfamiliar terms, and concepts in all the other curriculum areas. With this tremendous vocabulary load, he doesn't have time to learn each new word on sight, and must depend on phonics and word analysis techniques to help him identify unknown words quickly without losing the context.

If the child is "exposed" to English language reading materials at home, and sees his parents reading newspapers, magazines, and books, he is more inclined to want to try the reading activities for himself. Children of bilingual homes might have serious reading problems. There would be no English spoken at home to provide exposure to language experiences which help build vocabulary, and there would be a dearth of reading materials printed in English. These children then are actually "language deprived." They need an abundance of school reading and language experiences, drills, and reinforcement, and many language-oriented opportunities to counterbalance the home environment.

New concepts for sounding are introduced at different grade levels. A few students are ready for phonics instruction in first grade, but many are ready in second, and far more in third. Initial consonant sounds are taught in the first year, after the basic sight vocabulary has been introduced, and while the teacher is working on visual and auditory training. At this stage, the child has had experiences with words and has come to notice their irregularities and inconsistencies, so he understands and is ready to accept the need for phonics instruction. But ability to hear sounds and make the connection between sounds and letters varies, so your slower students or those with reading disabilities will need much more drill. For this reason, initial sounds are taught the first year, but are retaught the following years to ensure finding those students who need extra practice or who never learned the sounds. Phonics from previous years must be continuously reinforced.

Five Steps in Teaching Phonics

There is a definite order in teaching phonics. The basic steps are: (1) beginning consonants, (2) short vowel sounds, (3) ending consonants, (4) consonant blends, and (5) long vowel sounds.

(1) *Beginning consonants (initial consonants).* A consonant is a sound produced when the outgoing breath is squeezed or stopped somewhere between the throat and lips while making sounds other than those represented by the vowels, a, e, i, o, u. They can never be pronounced in isolation but must be followed by a vowel, otherwise the sound becomes a consonant plus "uh."

Initial consonant sounds can be taught in any order, but are usually based on utility—that is, how often the sound is used in daily experiences. At readiness level, the usual order is: *b, c, d, f, h, l, m, r, s, t.* At the pre-primer level these are reinforced, and the hard *g* and *w* sound are introduced; at primer level, reinforcement plus addition of *k, v, y, z* is emphasized. Auditory awareness of the two sounds for *c* and *g* are not introduced until second reader, level one, when the term "consonant" is introduced. Note that there are a few sounds that will occur *only* in initial position: these are *h, qu, w, wh,* and *y.* It is a good idea to check phonics comprehension with each remedial student before initiating his individual program.

(2) *Short vowel sounds.* It must be noted here that my order of presentation is *not* usually given in most reading guides.

Some authors suggest introducing initial and final consonants at first reader level, but don't advocate introduction of short vowel sounds until the second reader. In view of the fact that consonant sounds cannot be pronounced alone, but must always be preceded or followed by a vowel sound, it makes more sense to teach short vowels at the same time you are teaching initial and final consonants; otherwise students might acquire the habit of saying "buh," "duh," "puh," etc.

In our local school district we use the method of teaching initial consonants, then short vowels, so that students may hear the sound correctly in context. Cordts[1] also recommends introducing vowel sounds at this stage.

The usual order of presentation is exactly as given—*a, e, i, o, u,*—and then *y* and *w*. When introducing vowels, the teacher should introduce only one at a time, and reinforce with a "key word" on the chalkboard, employing many visual and auditory cues for reinforcement. For instance, if the key word is "b*a*t," she would teach or reinforce short *a* sound; the teacher could show a baseball bat while talking about the game, draw a bat on the chalkboard, read a story about baseball, and even *play* baseball with students during physical education period, and all of these activities would reinforce short *a* sound. Whenever possible, especially with remedial students, positive reinforcement techniques which afford success should be used. Also, by incorporating the key word into several curriculum areas, the teacher increases the amount of drill.

While the sound is *introduced* at this time, remember that much visual and auditory training is necessary before the student is ready to begin the writing stage. The key word is in front of the child as a visual discrimination aid, but the main emphasis is on the *auditory* cue.

---

[1] Anna D. Cordts, *PHONICS for the Reading Teacher* (New York: Holt, Rinehart and Winston, Inc., 1965).

Many auditory activities are necessary so the child hears the sound correctly and pronounces it correctly with its preceding consonant sound. Singing games, rhyming activities, nursery rhymes, guessing games, and riddles can be used.

This is also the time to start the oral initial consonant substitution drill. For instance, start with *b* at, and elicit from the students: *c* at, *h* at, *f* at, etc.

(Consonants are split apart here for your convenience. Do not split the sound when presenting such substitutions to your students. It will produce a distorted speech sound, something to be avoided at all costs.)

From the oral drill, you can then proceed to the chalkboard stage, and the experience charts. Many visual and auditory cues should be used, such as pictures, records, and music, and walks around the school yard on "discovery trips," so that the child experiences the use of language as sounds in his everyday life.

(3) *Final consonants.* Young children (and most adults) speak predominantly in monosyllables, using a kind of "verbal shorthand." Most conversations follow this general pattern. (Try it on your own speech habits—you'll see what I mean.) Therefore it is logical and most useful to introduce consonants in final position in one-syllable words.

Both children and adults tend to slur the ending sounds of words in their everyday speech, and this distorts the speech sounds. Teachers should be especially careful to pronounce the final consonants clearly, so that the child has a correct model.

Since most of the consonants can occur in initial or final position (*only* the blend *ng* will occur only in final position in the English language), a definite order of presentation is not mandatory, so the author feels introduction of final consonants should be based on *utility.* Build on the students' own prior experience and use words in their personal vocabulary and from the classroom environment. As stated earlier, you can tie these words to lessons given in other curriculum areas, as further reinforcement.

This is especially important with older remedial students

(upper grades), where the vocabulary load is so heavy. By stressing a basic sound, and using it repeatedly throughout the day, the student then begins to understand the correlation between letter name and letter sound, and can then use this knowledge to "unlock" unknown new words.

The most common sounds to begin teaching are *k, p,* and *t.* The *k* in loo*k,* wor*k,* for*k,* par*k* is usually introduced at primer level. The *p* sound in u*p,* hel*p,* ca*p,* and so on, and the *t* sound in ma*t,* fa*t,* le*t,* etc. are also used, as these words are already in the children's vocabulary. They follow the principle of using monosyllabic words. It is wise to avoid teaching "r" in final position in early lessons. This sound varies considerably due to regional accents or inflections. It also seems to be one of the most difficult sounds for a child to pronounce correctly. The sound of "r" should be delayed until the first reader level.

The same kinds of games, experiences, and exercises that you used for teaching and reinforcement for initial consonants can be adapted to teach final consonant position. Rhyming games are especially useful. Include many visual and auditory activities to strengthen remedial students' discrimination and configuration techniques.

(4) *Blends.* There are two circumstances in which two or more consonants occur together at the beginning of a word. These are consonant blends and consonant digraphs.

A consonant blend is a blend in which the sounds of both letters are heard, such as the *b* and *l* in *bl*ack, or the *s* and *t* in *st*ory. A *digraph* occurs when two consonants appear together, but make an entirely different sound from the one each makes when heard alone: for example *t* alone as in *t*ea, *h* alone as in *h*e, but together makes a new sound such as *th* in *th*is, *th*ese, *th*ose, and yet another sound in *th*ink, *th*in, and *th*ick.

In actual teaching practice, the digraphs *wh, ch,* and *th* are usually introduced before teaching blends, as they occur frequently in the basic sight vocabulary and in everyday speech. However, after the introduction, both blends and digraphs can be taught together. Both require giving much visual and auditory instruction.

The usual order of introduction for blends is *bl, br, dr, fl, fr, gr, pl, st,* and *tr* at the first reader level, and *ch, th,* and *wh* for digraphs. Blends and digraphs should always be taught with the adjacent vowel sound, as you do with single consonants, and for the same reason—they cannot be heard in isolation.

(5) *Long vowels.* Short and long vowels should never be taught at the same time. The introduction to long vowel sounds is usually delayed because of the spelling problems. An example is the use of "silent e" on the end of a word, which makes the preceding vowel long, and the use of a vowel digraph such as the *ea* in m*ea*t or the *oa* in b*oa*t. Long vowel sounds and digraphs are taught at the end of the first reader or beginning second reader level, when students have mastered initial and final consonants, and short vowel sounds and blends.

Before beginning remedial instruction in long vowel sounds, a nonsense word spelling test should be given to check students' mastery of initial and final consonants, blends and short vowel sounds. On page 58 is a good representative list from which to make up your own test.

When should the teaching of phonics begin?

How important is mental age in judging phonics readiness?

There are almost as many conflicting opinions on this issue as there were in the sight versus sound controversy. General opinion is that most children are ready for phonics instruction in first grade. However, this author does not agree with that.

Phonics instruction can be initiated at *kindergarten* level. The teacher can provide many and varied experiences in visual and auditory discrimination to sharpen her students' *awareness* of sounds. Starting at this level, we take advantage of the child's initial enthusiasm for school and of most children's desire to learn to read. Indeed, some of these youngsters enter kindergarten expecting to learn to read the first day! Why not take advantage of this and use it to the utmost?

Of course, many children will *not* be ready for this stage and to force them beyond their maturity level could prove harmful to later development of reading skills. But I must emphasize that individualization or small group instruction is still the key. Therefore, some children will be "ready" for phonics at this stage, but *all* will benefit from these visual-auditory experiences.

NONSENSE WORDS

dup	lek	neb	vazwib	kotlup
nim	rop	kes	nedwil	mitvar
bod	mab	seb	hutlik	rusteb
mib	daz	gep	sektap	polnim
lup	pag	fub	kelnab	tumrak
wep	lat	pab	weskon	takpul
dep	rup	ref	tikrep	muplod

Here is a list of nonsense words the teacher can use to make up a nonsense word spelling test, to check understanding of consonants in initial and final position, and of short vowel sounds. Later on, the two syllable nonsense words at the end of the list can be used to check beginning word analysis syllabication, and consonants in medial position. These are only representative samples, and should be added to by the classroom teacher. Do not give a very long test; about sixteen words (combining one and two syllable combinations) should be adequate for diagnosis.

Figure 4-1

5

Perception – the Unknown Quantity, and How to Measure It in Reading

This chapter and the one immediately following are concerned with perception. The difference in the two chapters is in degree. This chapter will touch on all areas of sensory perception and give an overview of how they affect a child's learning, while Chapter 6 will concentrate on dyslexia, or word blindness, as a more severe type of reading disability.

In this chapter we will be primarily concerned with perceptual handicaps that are not particularly severe and which the classroom teacher can help alleviate. While most classroom teachers do not have the experience, training, or time to devote to actual perceptual training, there are many activities a dedicated teacher can employ to stimulate and strengthen perceptual areas. Indeed, I have found that my entire class benefits from perceptual exercises and activities which can easily be adapted for use with individuals or small groups.

Perceptual difficulties, as explained in Chapter 2, manifest themselves by causing different types of behavior and in different degrees according to the severity of the handicap.

A student suspected of a perceptual problem must be watched both in the classroom and on the playground. His physical activities, body movements, and behavior provide clues to perceptual problems. Some of the symptoms of perceptual disability are awkward movements in playground games, clumsy walking or running, and poor control on playground gym equipment. In the classroom the student exhibits poor cutting, folding, or pasting skills, and makes number, letter, and figure reversals. For example, I had one child who could never find the right place in her textbooks, because she reversed the numbers. She read 26 for 62, or 69 for 96, etc. Another student usually helped her find the correct page in the book.

A child with a perceptual handicap will show reluctance to participate in any new activity. He may not want to try any new exercise which involves using new motions or unfamiliar tools; and he will hang back in new games, physical education exercises, and will only want to participate in activities he has experienced before and for which he knows the routine.

On suspicion of a perceptual disability, the teacher should test to determine type and magnitude, and then corrective techniques can be instituted. Remember that the method of correction is determined by the type of disability.

Causes of Perceptual Handicaps

A good working definition of perception is "the interpretation of sensation." Perception is based on previous experiences of sensation through interaction with the environment.

The exact causes of perceptual handicaps are difficult to establish. Doctors disagree as to general causes. As the disorders themselves exhibit different clinical symptoms, so do the causes differ. No one seems to be able to say positively that certain factors will generate certain perceptual difficulties. Doctors and psychologists *suspect* these factors as possibly attributing to the disorders: (1) minimal brain damage before, during, or immediately after birth, (2) genetic factors or hereditary afflictions, (3) mental retardation (which can be due to a variety of causes), (4) cross dominance, (5) malnutrition before or after birth, (6) certain vitamin deficiencies, (7) chemical imbalance in the child's body chemistry, (8) side effects from prenatal medications, (9) certain food additives and preservatives, especially the red dyes used in luncheon meats, weiners, etc., and (10) certain types of lighting. More research is being done in this area, and side effects of many of these causes are currently under investigation.

We are becoming more aware that few human beings are born perfect or develop perfectly. The job of teachers, therefore, is not only the task of teaching, but now also one of identifying and correcting handicaps, as best they can.

Six Sensory Modes and How They Affect Perception

Most people are born with the six sensory modes intact. These modes are: vision, hearing, touch, taste, smell, and kinesthis (muscle sense).

Perception should not be confused with sensation. Perception is the use and interpretation of the sensory modes based on prior experiences. Sensation, then, is the result of perception. Since it is learned, it can be taught using planned exercises and activities.

"Perception," per se, is still a relatively new field and the full extent of its effects on reading and language skills has not been fully explored, but we can identify it and we can concern ourselves with treating the associated reading disabilities and behavioral disorders which fall within the purview of the classroom teacher.

(1) *Vision.* One of the senses most people take for granted is vision. Visual perception is *not* the same thing as vision. Vision is how an object *looks,* the real image. Perception is the brain's interpretation of how an object looks or is seen by the

individual. Sometimes a distorted or incomplete picture is "transmitted" to the brain through the body's communication network. When this happens, and a child perceives (interprets) differently, his visual cues to reading are short-circuited.

With such students, some of the visual-perceptual disabilities you may notice are letter or number reversals (the most common) in writing; figure-ground disability (where the child cannot pick out the central figure against a background); visual sequential memory, in which a child cannot remember a sequence of letters in a word; visual closure, where a figure or word is incomplete (the child only perceives part of the figure).

As an example, in a visual closure handicap, persons with normal visual perception would see a whole object, but the child with a disability would "see" only part of the object. This may be reflected in his drawings or in the way he colors them. Backgrounds may be incomplete and human figures may be distorted or have parts of the bodies missing. In writing or copying, words will be incomplete, with parts of the letters or even of whole phrases missing.

Watch children's figures when they are drawing or cutting. When these figures are incomplete or have misplaced arms and legs, you can suspect that the child has inadequate visual closure. For instance, our school bulletin board had on display cut-out pictures of snowmen done by a kindergarten class. These figures were complete with top hats, mufflers, belts, etc., cut from colored construction paper. Two of the snowmen showed strong indications of visual closure disability. On one figure, the brim of the top hat was missing, the face was placed quite a bit off-center, and the eyebrows were not above the eyes, but off to the sides. On the other cut-out drawing, the top part of the snowman (chest) was much larger than the bottom, and the bottom part was misshapen and elongated. In addition, the arms and hands were attached to the bottom part of the figure, below the belt line. Both these young artists should have been tested for visual-perceptual disabilities, and remediation instituted as soon as possible.

A figure-ground disability might be compared to a movie

film, where the figures and objects in the background are fuzzy and indistinct. You are aware that they are there, but the dominant image is the figure at the front of the screen. A child with figure-ground disability does not have the other images recede into the background, leaving the dominant image intact. Therefore, the picture becomes confused and the child is unable to interpret it properly.

Recently, a television program in San Francisco presented a young man, an artist, who could not hold a job. While he could draw and paint beautifully, even execute architectural design, he had one problem—he couldn't read! All letters in signs, and on printed pages were reversed. His "perception" of letters and numbers was from right to left. This was the image his brain received.

He also had difficulty driving a car because he couldn't interpret the freeway signs fast enough. By the time he read the sign, reversed the letters mentally and interpreted the message it presented, he had driven past the correct lane or exit!

Perceptual constancy is the ability to perceive that an object will have certain characteristics that do not change, regardless of the position or angle from which it is viewed. This involves size, shape, color, texture, and so on. A person with a visual perceptual handicap may perceive a figure one way in one context, but it might have a totally different interpretation when viewed in another situation. This distortion will definitely affect the child's interpretation in reading.

As an example, a normally perceiving person viewing a moving car from a distance will perceive the car as having the same size and shape not only as it comes toward him, but as it moves away. However, if the car is observed from *above* but approximately the same distance away, the car may appear smaller! And to a handicapped person, all *three* views of the object might appear different. He might even interpret them as being three different cars!

John F., an army clerk, became very tired and would get violent headaches after working several hours on routine printed matter. Often, he would become nauseated after typing long lists. One day, while looking at a chart on the wall, he asked another clerk, "How many figures do you see on that top line?"

"Why, two," was the reply.

John saw four, two of each of the numbers! He had double vision, which meant the images were not fusing in the brain centers. After discovering the disability for himself, he sought professional help. An ophthalmologist who specialized in treatment of visual perceptual handicaps prescribed special training exercises. Daily vision exercises helped John overcome his handicap.

To the teacher familiar only with her "normal" perspective, a visual perceptual problem is difficult to appreciate. We seem to take it for granted that all people "see" alike.

A fast way to test a child you suspect may have a figure-ground perceptual handicap is the following: Stand with the youngster at a window. Have him describe what he sees, telling you where each object is located. Example: Where is the tree? Where is the bench, near or far away? Which is closer? etc. Have the child locate buildings, trees, and other things in relation to other objects.

You can also use this method with pictures, and have the student locate objects in the picture, and relate them to other objects, using such terms as near-far, up-down, top-bottom, etc. With very young children, picture books are a good source, while with older students, books with photographs are excellent. In art class, studies of paintings by famous artists can be utilized.

The idea that anyone, particularly a child, may suffer from distorted or static-ridden impressions and images, is stunning, on first exposure. The teacher must become empathetic to the child whose facilities are under development and who, somehow, is not getting and interpreting the sensory signals properly. "As the twig is bent . . ." has profound meaning when applied here.

(2) *Hearing.* A child with a disability in auditory perception does not interpret sounds as others do. Indeed, many times what we hear as certain sounds are to this child just "noise." He

is unable to effectively screen out background noises which interfere with his perception of sounds related to tasks at hand. In some cases, certain sounds cannot even be perceived. He may be poor in spelling, and when given the oral spelling of a word, can't remember it long enough to return to his desk and write it down. This child is easily distracted, and may get letters and syllables of words reversed or twisted. He may have a history of delayed speech in infancy and will probably be poor in phonics, because he can't remember sounds long enough to blend them into a word. He may have difficulty learning street names, can't remember his phone number, and will have difficulty counting and learning the alphabet.

To check auditory discrimination, the teacher should give the child a series of instructions (two or three), and observe to see if he can remember them long enough to carry them out, in order. If auditory perception difficulties are suspected, have the school nurse or school psychologist follow up with a professional test to discover the exact nature and severity of the handicap.

Several years ago, I had a student who was unable to hear separate sounds in spoken words. For this youngster, phonics instruction was virtually useless. After conferencing with the mother, we discovered this was a genetic disorder which she also suffered. As a child, she had also been poor in phonics, and only learned to read by memorizing the words as "sight words." She was sympathetic to her son's disability, and was willing to help in any way possible. Visual instruction and the visual perceptual channels provided the most effective means of instruction in the beginning. The Dolch Basic Sight Word List was used to reinforce visual channels, and at the same time instruction and therapy was instituted in auditory channels. The child was taught to listen for sounds, such as how many times a ball bounced, while actually watching the ball. Later, we had him turn his back and count the number of times the ball bounced. We had him listen to records involving sounds of animals and sounds on city streets. Then we worked with sounds of the letters, but introduced and reinforced only one at a time. We concentrated on finding many words which had the "target" sound, and gave many visual clues to take advantage of the visual channel strength while working on the auditory channel. By this stimuli association, we were able to alleviate part of the disability.

Some types of auditory disabilities are caused by lack of language experience, i.e., not enough verbal expression in early childhood. They can also be the result of a speech handicap, such as a lisp, or can be neurologically based. Most can be helped through exercises emphasizing verbal expression.

Jean M. entered my class with a definite reading-language disability. When sounding out words, she hesitated, stumbled over many consonant sounds, enunciating incorrectly, and was unable to pronounce some sounds at all. On investigation, I discovered that she was the youngest of five children. As the youngest, she was petted and "babied" by her brothers and sisters. They would feed her, give her cookies, or hand her toys, without her needing to ask for them. With no need for talking, Jean didn't! Consequently, the soft palate, tongue, etc., were not exercised sufficiently nor forced to make the proper sounds.

Children such as Jean can be helped through exercises emphasizing verbal expression. (In extreme cases, such as this one, speech therapy is also necessary.) Children love to "pretend," and so puppet plays, finger play, singing games, and "Show and Tell" help children develop channels of auditory perception.

(3) *Touch.* Very young children are tactilely oriented. They like to feel things, and it is important to their security. Babies derive comfort from the feel of warm cuddly blankets and soft toys, and children cling to the hands of their teachers for the security given in the sense of touch. For most of them, it is their "first step" away from home and with outside contact with grown-up strangers. They must learn to identify with these adults.

A child with a neurological behavioral disorder will use this sense to "lash out" against a world which he doesn't understand. This child's disability may stem from a visual or auditory perceptual problem, but manifests itself behaviorally by the child's activities involving touch. He is restless, and can't sit and concentrate effectively for any length of time. He may pull another child's hair, tweak his ear in passing, mark on another child's paper, and frequently destroys others' belongings. On the playground, the child appears hyperactive, and runs wildly. His games involve hitting or tripping others. He is free with his fists, and when feeling oppressed or cornered, is apt to pick up a rock as a retaliatory measure. He knows better, but just can't seem to help himself. He has great difficulty "keeping his hands and feet to himself." How do we help him? How do we control his behavior?

Doctors now believe part of this behavior may be due to a chemical imbalance or dysfunction in the child. It could be likened to the energy level "spilling over" in the brain, causing increased body activity, similar to the way convulsive attacks would affect an epileptic. The child actually has more energy than he knows what to do with; consequently, his increased motor activity will result in erratic motor control behavior.

Physicians now believe some of these behavioral disabilities can be controlled by use of certain drugs (chemotherapy), which will affect the child's body chemistry. If the aberrant behavior can be controlled by drugs prescribed by the child's physician during the formative years (usually until puberty), then his motor control processes can be adequately channeled until he develops patterns of self-discipline and effective behavior.

Tasks involving manipulative materials will help this child channel his energy. An example of this is a "Feelie Box": Take a cardboard carton that still has the lid flaps attached. Decorate the entire carton, then cut a small hole in the center of one side. (Leave one flap open at the back so that articles may be placed in the box. Choose articles for the Feelie Box that vary in size, shape, and texture. The child reaches into the small front opening, grasps an article, describes its shape, texture, etc., and then confirms his guess when the teacher removes the article via the flap in the back of the box. Many games can be devised using the Feelie Box to provide more tactile experiences. When working with hyperactive children, change tasks often at first, due to the child's short attention span. Then gradually work toward longer manipulative tasks to strengthen his self-control. In addition, extra personal attention (counseling and guidance) is always effective.

(4) *Taste.* Children never take the taste of food for granted, and during early years seem to lead a "hand to mouth" existence, tasting most objects in their environment (including dirt). This perceptual sense involves lips, teeth, tongue, soft and hard palate, and the process of chewing and swallowing. These are also involved in the speech processes, and it seems reasonable to expect that proper development of the taste function should affect perceptual channels, and in fact many speech disabilities are caused by improper development or use of these parts.

Where mild disabilities exist, teachers can assist in speech training by providing stimulating classroom experiences. Meals can be discussed and children encouraged to talk about favorite foods and how they taste. The class can all eat lunch together as an activity and can discuss lunches and good table manners. Who can forget the smell of a peanut butter sandwich? A "tasting box" can be arranged where children can identify different tastes, such as sweet, salty, sour, and bitter. The box should include items normally found in the child's lunch box or in his home environment. All these experiences will stimulate a child's perception of taste, and this sense can be capitalized on in language discussions and creative writing activities.

(5) *Smell.* Taste and smell are closely related. One enhances and reinforces the other. Without the sense of smell most objects would taste only sweet, salty, sour, or bitter. It is the sense of smell which makes the bacon sizzling on the stove appealing, and freshly-baked cookies disappear so quickly from their racks where they are cooling.

Perhaps it is strange to discuss gustatory activities in a book on remedial reading, but again, many stimulating creative

activities should be used to sharpen the disabled child's awareness and his use of the senses.

A "smelling box," like the one set up for taste, with
samples of different types of foods, spices, etc. can be utilized
to stimulate creative writing activities and to help develop the
perception of sense of smell. From a smelling box, children can
be taught to remember how a freshly-mowed lawn smells, or an
apple, or even the diesel fumes from the school bus. In my
classroom the children even notice and comment on the smell
of the ink in our wide-tipped felt pens used to make charts and
drawings.

All these types of activities should be used wherever
possible.

(6) *Kinesthesis (muscle sense)*. A child with poor concepts of
body image will have difficulty with many classroom activities.
His concept of his position in space is poor, and he may be poor
at sports (not always), or appear clumsy, slow, and awkward in
movement. On the playground, he will have difficulty with
running, skipping, and throwing and catching a ball, and has
difficulty remembering left and right, misjudges when moving
around furniture, bumps into objects, and may misjudge the
height of steps and stumble when moving up and down a flight.
In drawing, his figures will be incomplete or parts of arms and
legs will stem from wrong parts of the body, or be missing
altogether, and the artwork will appear dull and lifeless. Usually
the drawing will consist of one or two figures, and will have
little "background" material in the landscapes.

The student may also have difficulty with large and small
muscle activities, such as cutting and pasting in art. He becomes
easily frustrated and doesn't want to finish these projects
involving motor control.

Jay L., a student in my class, had extreme difficulty
learning to cut snowflakes for a classroom project. He could not
control the scissors, and clumsily tried to feed the paper into
the scissors, causing it to crumple and tear. He couldn't hold the
scissors correctly, nor could he fold the paper circle to have six
sides, even with repeated demonstrations. Finally, with much

help, Jay learned to hold scissors correctly, and to cut out figures to his personal satisfaction. It is my opinion that in most cases, school scissors are inadequate and inefficient. Therefore, remediation for Jay included the use of my large teacher's shears under close adult supervision. Also, at home Jay was allowed to practice cutting paper and cloth with large scissors.

A child with a kinesthetic disability will frequently have poor handwriting, and his papers are usually messy and torn; erasures are frequent. Most of the time, he will be unable to complete a written assignment, sometimes is only able to put down one or two words on the paper.

This child needs to find his position in space—to locate himself. He must become aware of his body parts and how they are integrated. The child must learn to relate himself to the objects around him (his environment).

Training activities to strengthen weak areas are the body skills: running, jumping; hopping activities: skipping, hopping on one foot (the teacher should designate—left or right foot). Later on, small muscle activities, such as bead stringing, learning to cut properly with scissors, origami (paper folding), can be utilized. Any game or activity that involves watching simple motor control activities and then imitating them is useful. "Follow the Leader" is an excellent game for this type of child. Balancing games and balancing equipment are also effective.

Most youngsters need to sharpen their awareness of their bodies and how to control them effectively. Therefore, these motor skills activities should not be limited to children with gross motor control dysfunction, but should be used with *all* the children in your class.

Simple jigsaw puzzles, block games, and all tactilely-oriented games can be utilized. They are beneficial to all children, and are excellent rainy day activities. In addition, games like Seven Up, King and Queen, Dog and the Bone are excellent "quiet games" for rainy days, to help students learn to move quietly and to balance using different parts of their bodies. (See Chapter 10.)

Types of Visual Perceptual Techniques for Remediation

Since we are concerned with remedial reading, the techniques and activities described here are oriented toward strengthening the visual perceptual channels. These activities will include use of some commercial materials and also others the teacher can devise or make.

Usually a child with a visual perceptual handicap will become audio- or tactilely-oriented. He will want to use these "strong" channels to compensate for his weakened visual perceptual skill. Specialists are of two opinions on remediating in this area. Do we let the child use the stronger skills, and learn to depend on these channels, or do we find ways to improve the weaker visual perceptual channel?

It is actually better to use *both* channels at once—employing many hand-eye activities. By coordinating both channels of "input," we can take advantage of the stronger area to help train in the weaker one. The activities described here will utilize and capitalize on this method.

For audio-oriented children, take advantage of your story hour. All children enjoy listening when the teacher reads aloud. Pick a story or book with a sequence of events. Read the story or part of the book, then play a guessing game. Have the students tell the story back to you, and see how many events they can tell in proper sequence. This can be used with a small group of remedial students, or as an entire class activity. Most children, especially in primary grades, need more practice in sequencing. This is an excellent activity for the entire class, to help develop this skill.

Visual Sequential Memory: If a child has difficulty remembering the sequence of letters in a word, or gets syllables reversed, can't remember numbers in a pattern, then these clues are all symptomatic of a disability in the visual perceptual channel. To strengthen this channel, any types of activities which follow a definite pattern are recommended. For younger students, "dot-to-dot" activities, using both those with letters of the alphabet or numbers in sequence are very good, and the children like them. (It is also an excellent way to reinforce alphabetical sequence for the remedial students having difficulty with the concept.)

"Dot-to-dots" using numbers are also useful to strengthen mathematical concepts. After the children have mastered simple numerical facts, you can use "dot-to-dots" which *start* with 101, 102, 103, etc., to teach place value concepts, especially the idea of using zero as a place holder in three digit numbers. Many students have difficulty with this concept, not just the remedial students, or those with perceptual problems, so this exercise lends itself well to entire group activities.

Another activity students enjoy is working a "maze." Mazes fascinate children, and are useful in teaching orientation in space. They are also valuable in remediating figure-ground disabilities. A similar activity is the "hidden picture." In these, there are usually several picture forms embedded in a larger over-all picture. The students find the small pictured forms hidden in the drawings, and then can color the picture. Many children's magazines publish these as activities and some of the best examples are those in *Highlights*[1] magazine. Simple puzzle pictures where all the forms are alike but one, and the student finds the different ones are excellent remedial activities.

The classroom teacher cannot *treat* perceptual disorders as such, and should leave diagnosis and remediation to specialists. However, the exercises and perceptual training activities given in this chapter will help students to compensate for perceptual disabilities.

Any child with a perceptual disability will have difficulty learning and will become easily frustrated and discouraged. Since these youngsters *do* become frustrated and nervous, activities should be easy, fun, and relaxing. Plan exercises that strengthen weak channels while providing success. As strength-

---

[1] *Highlights for Children, Inc.,* 2300 West Fifth Ave., Columbus, Ohio 43216.

ening one channel usually will transfer to other channels, strengthening and reinforcing them, also, incorporate into your remedial program exercises and activities that will strengthen all perceptual channels, and help the student learn to use all six sensory modes to the utmost of his ability.

Individualization

At this point we can now picture a classroom of some 20 or 30 children. As their bright, expectant faces come into focus we suddenly realize that we are not looking at an oversized human pea pod.

As we become familiar with the children, some begin to isolate themselves in our awareness as individuals with problems out of the ordinary, each unique. Hopefully, as we test and observe, the specific problem of each student and its cause becomes known to us.

Since each child's problem is unique, it will require an individualization of treatment, and in an "ordinary" classroom, this is a juggling act that makes five balls in the air look easy.

In later chapters we will attack the problem of individualization in a comprehensive way, but we still have one fascinating subject to cover: Dyslexia.

6

Dyslexia –
What Is It, How Do We Spot It,
and Remedial Approaches You Can Take

According to physicians, "dyslexia" refers to specific disability in reading. Dyslexia can:

(1) Cause a person to read the background of a printed page, rather than the printing.

(2) Cause a person to read from right to left, rather than left to right.

(3) Cause a person to "see" only part of a word; instead of reading 'reply,' he will read re———, or ——ply, or re——y.

As much as 5 percent of our *total* population is estimated as having dyslexia, a Minimal Cerebral Dysfunction which interferes with reading, or which causes difficulty during the person's school career. This is probably a conservative estimate, considering there are 21,000,000 functionally illiterate persons in the United States at the present time. Many of these are probably adult dyslexics who were not discovered or diagnosed during their formative, early years. The entire field of research in dyslexia, per se, is comparatively new, most of it having developed over the past 20 years. (Among my adult friends, I personally know of at least two who are diagnosed dyslexics, and have difficulty reading. Both were high school dropouts due to difficulties in reading.)

The classic symptoms of dyslexia (or word blindness) are reversals in reading and writing, poorly established cerebral dominance resulting in confusion in selection of correct images during reading, stuttering or stammering, and ambilaterality (poor manipulation and confusion as to parts of the body, particularly differentiation between left and right hand—left and right foot.)

As with most perceptual disabilities, dyslexia is a matter of degree, and severe dyslexic children cannot be remediated in the classroom. These children suffer from other related disabilities and need special attention to help them overcome personal, social, and emotional disabilities incurred with their dyslexia. Such problems are beyond the range of the classroom teacher, and if she suspects a child to be severely dyslexic, immediate referral is recommended. Less severe dyslexics can be helped in the classroom by use of visual, audial and motor training exercises and activities.

To help us understand the dyslexic child and to enable us to benefit from his reactions to his disability, it is necessary for us to be clinical about his behavior. Therefore, let us spend some time on categorizing behavior.

Levels of Human Effectiveness—How Dyslexics Perform

Each person meets the challenges and frustrations of everyday life according to his own personal, social, and emotional needs. He copes with his environment, and the situations that develop therein, by use of his experiential background and his perception of himself and others.

A dyslexic child will meet his challenges by coping with the problem situation just as others do, but will experience deeper feelings of frustration and anxiety due to his inadequate perceptual skills, and his inability to communicate these feelings to those around him: his parents, his teachers, and his classmates. He usually reacts to the difficulty imposed by feeling rage, by crying, or by withdrawal. His method of handling the situation and his feelings about himself are functions of his own personality and are indicative of his personal needs.

According to Lister[1], there are five levels of human effectiveness: (1) panic, (2) inertia, (3) striving, (4) coping, and (5) mastery.

(1) *Panic* occurs when a child is threatened or feels threatened by the environment. In severe dyslexics the child might exhibit autistic behavior and need institutional care for self-protection. He loses self-control to a degree that he endangers himself and others.

(2) *Inertia.* At this level the child exerts little control over his own environment. He remains passive, apathetic, and can't respond to immediate problems or to situations. He is not goal-oriented, and can't organize behavior patterns. He depends on others to organize behavior and is usually "outer-directed." He passively submits to events around him, making no effort to modify his own behavior or his environment.

(3) *Striving.* A striving child has fair control over his own emotions and his reactions, and he is able to work on difficult problems before frustration sets in. This child meets each crisis as it occurs, usually "head on." He does not plan ahead nor organize his environment to meet long-term goals. Usually he can identify with his peers, but

---

[1] James L. Lister, *Teacher Diagnosis of Educational Differences*, ed. by Robert M. Smith (Columbus, Ohio: Charles E. Merrill Publishing Co., 1969), p. 173.

sees himself as "different." His feeling of self-worth is usually precarious, and his relationship with adults and his peers reflects his feelings of uncertainty about himself.

(4) *Coping*. At this level of development, the child works actively to change his environment. He is capable of long-range planning and views life as a challenge. He may appear highly efficient, and well-organized on the surface, but still may have feelings of uncertainty about himself (anxiety). At this level the child is never quite convinced he is accepted by his peers. His feelings of success are sometimes overcome by his anxiety and striving behavior.

(5) *Mastery*. Very few individuals of any age attain this state for any length of time. People are always striving toward mastery along a continuum. This type of personality plans and executes long-range goals successfully and also responds to immediate challenges within his environment. He meets life with feelings of adequacy, security, and mastery much of the time. To him, living is fun. He has a strong positive self-image and identifies with his peers, but doesn't depend on them.

The severely dyslexic child will seldom attain the final two levels, and will have extreme difficulty functioning at the striving level.

In the past, we have been prone to label students as lazy or energetic, bright or dull, honest or dishonest, moral or immoral (bright children were generally considered to be honest and moral)—simplistic titles that enabled *us* to be lazy, dull, dishonest and ?? Primarily the labeling allowed us to be negligent. Problem students were swiftly relegated to the status of creatures fated to worthlessness, a category which assured their being given the vast amount of inattention and derision required to make them exactly that.

We can no longer do this. Alas, we have learned that aberrant behavior is a symptom of emotional, physical, and psychological problems, and knowing this, we have no excuse for ignoring the behavior, but must search for the cause.

One of the causes is dyslexia. By judging a child's level of effectiveness, we can begin to determine whether or not he may be dyslexic. By observing his behavior, we can gather further evidence to help evaluate his disability.

Personal, Social, and Emotional Factors and How They Affect Learning

With levels of effectiveness in mind, look around your classroom for signs of aberrant behavior. Remember that most students will behave abnormally some of the time as part of their efforts at coping with situations. This is part of a normal growth pattern. However, if a student exhibits several of these behavioral symptoms, closer observation is justified. They may be "hidden" dyslexics.

Dishonesty—This category includes cheating, lying, and stealing. If the child cheats on written work, looking on other students' papers, or putting answers where he can copy them, or takes things from other students' desks, then this is symptomatic of a deeper need. The child doesn't feel adequate on his own, and is exhibiting coping, striving behavior. Also, if he consistently lies about small things, especially concerning himself and his behavior toward others, this may be a clue to emotional handicaps.

Laziness—This child is unwilling to perform as he should or could. Rather than do his work, he will sit and play with his pencil or talk with neighbors. He might also use the old ploy, "Teacher, can I do something to help you?" This child can also be clever at finding tasks which take him away from classroom activities. For instance, he will deliberately walk in mud, so that he can stay outside the classroom to "clean the mud off my shoes." Or he will suddenly need to clean out his desk, and organize it so he can find his work papers. These are examples of coping and inertia, escape mechanisms to take him away from the tasks at hand.

Withdrawal—This child doesn't interact with the teacher or with other students. He pulls back into his shell like a turtle, and sits watching the world go by. By observation I've noticed this type child usually tends to perseverate. Once he gets started working in one particular area, he cannot change tasks easily. He will actually "lose" himself in the activity on which he is working, to the extent of his entire surroundings. Many times, it will take three or four tries before he responds when you call on him. It might actually be necessary that you touch the child on the shoulder before you can get his attention.

This was the case with Richard, who was in one of my classes. He was a very brilliant boy, but had definite perceptual difficulty. He would sit hunched in his coat, with the parka hood pulled down to hide his face. Richard was never a discipline problem, but had difficulty completing written work due to his withdrawal. His inertia was such that he didn't like to go out for recess or P.E., preferring to stay in the classroom at his desk. His shoelaces were always loose, because at second grade he still "didn't know how to tie."

While observing Richard, I noticed he would take a piece of paper, make a few letters on it, then crumple it and throw it away. I discovered that Richard was a frustrated perfectionist. He wasn't satisfied with his own efforts, and thus would throw them away.

Further investigation revealed his hand-eye coordination was poor, as was his motor control, thus he couldn't make letters and numbers that closely approximated the models. Remediation for Richard consisted of tracking exercises, tracing over sandpaper letters, and dot-to-dots. His individual program consisted of personal attention, with myself or an aide *moving* Richard's hand and arm through the proper muscle coordination exercises. After several months of the training exercises, Richard himself could see that his writing and drawing were improving, and he became a much happier person.

Fatigue—This child appears to be tired all the time, and has difficulty getting through the entire school day. Usually there is no organic cause, and a physical examination verifies this, but the child will put his head down on his desk complaining of feeling tired, or will say, "Teacher, I don't feel well." Again this is an escape mechanism, evidence of the child's inability to cope with the situation. He is functioning at the inertia level of effectiveness.

Absenteeism—Many times this trait is a symptom the child is not functioning adequately in the classroom. He develops a headache or will feel sick to his stomach, and will convince himself *and* his parents that he is actually sick. In these cases, parental attitude is very important. If the child is allowed to stay home, he does not learn to cope with the environment and the school situation. He is functioning at the panic level. Conferences with parents would be a wise course to help the child surmount the panic level and learn to handle his problems. Both teacher and parents must be consistent in their attitude toward the child.

Over-identification with adults—This type of behavior on the part of a child is misleading. The child may actually appear to be very mature. He reacts well to adults and seems to live in an adult world. However, on closer inspection, he doesn't seem to have an identity of his own. He doesn't play much, and seems to need and derive comfort from the adult's presence.

Over-identification with peer groups—This student is dependent on others to fulfill his personal, social, and emotional needs. While identification with peers is a normal developmental stage, this child is overly dependent, and has no values of his own. He develops no sense of independence, and just "runs with the crowd," regardless of its behavior.

Disrespect for authority—"Everybody picks on me. Nobody likes me." This is the standard answer of this type of personality. This child refuses to accept rules or commands from adults, and yet when confronted with his unruly behavior responds by placing the blame elsewhere. He refuses to recognize the problem as being his own, and is functioning at the panic level.

Disrespect for property—Most of us have noticed students marking on books with their pencils or marking on the tops of desks, etc., which usually only indicates boredom. A dyslexic child will carry these qualities to extremes in his panic pattern. He not only will mark on books, table tops, and papers, but seems to actually *attack* the objects, hitting with his pencil. He will throw books and papers in the classroom, giving vent to his anger and frustration. When crossed, he retaliates by throwing and destroying everything within reach. He is operating very close to the panic level of effectiveness.

Also be alert for the other type of personality which exhibits this trait. *This* child surreptitiously damages property and is more withdrawn. He is less willing to be openly defiant, less willing to accept the consequences of his behavior. He feels inadequate, unable to cope with a world he finds frustrating and unjust. One manifestation of this type is the "pencil breaker," who breaks the leads or even the pencils, and the "eraser peeler," who either breaks, pokes holes in, or otherwise tears up his erasers, or will even pull the metal caps loose and destroy the eraser on his pencil.

Cruelty—This trait is related to the two categories just mentioned. Usually the child who destroys property and defies authority will also express overtly or covertly manifestations of cruelty. He may torment, tease, or attack younger children or animals, especially in a situation in which retaliation or punishment is unlikely. He will seldom get into situations requiring retaliation with children of his own age group, but if such a situation occurs, and the other child "hits back" or defends himself, the dyslexic child may cry or run away.

Keys to Classroom Appraisal

We have established levels of human effectiveness, and have shown that aberrant behavior *can* be symptomatic of dyslexia. However, normal children are often lazy and often behave abnormally for short periods because of temporary upsets in their homes and lives, so we need more than just observation to diagnose and treat dyslexia.

It is not improbable that everything being written about

dyslexia today will be obsolete before the ink is dry, because the "infant" field is growing rapidly. Numerous highly competent researchers arc active in the field, and a flood of material is becoming available. For the classroom teacher of today there are techniques and tests that provide the means for doing a very competent job of discovering and helping a dyslexic child.

Finding the dyslexic child with a diagnostic reading test is the initial step in any evaluation. Many of the perceptual handicaps overlap into other areas, so the teacher should evaluate the subtests in reading. After the diagnostic tests are completed and evaluated, the next step in finding M.C.D. handicaps is by classroom appraisal, i.e., an informal evaluation. By these measures, a teacher discovers the specific areas of weakness. Through three categories of sensory perception (visual, auditory, and motor control), and by classroom observation, he may be able to determine whether the problem is primarily caused by reception (intake), association (analogies), or feedback (output) weaknesses. This translates to: Does the child have difficulty seeing and interpreting the words, or does he have difficulty giving back the meaning of the material read?

Watch how the child holds his pencil and the way he draws and writes. Circles should start at one o'clock and be drawn counterclockwise. Straight lines should be drawn from top to bottom. If he starts straight lines at the line of the paper and moves his pencil upwards, he is moving it in the opposite direction to normal. This is a possible clue to both intake and feedback disability.

Check to see how well the child can copy or trace simple figures and diagrams. Where does he *start* on the drawing? Sometimes a child's difficulty in writing or motor skills is because he cannot transfer from spacial to temporal orientation, that is, in drawing a square or figure, he doesn't know where to begin, or which line or component should be drawn first, nor does he know where he should stop. There must be a match between the child's perception of the object (reception) and his own subsequent movements in drawing (feedback) for effective motor control to take place. He needs to exclude all non-pertinent perceptual data and screen out the unimportant background features of configuration.

Observe the technique with which the child forms words or letters when writing. Letters should be firm and strokes should be even, and combination letters (straight line and circle combinations) should meet. There should be no spaces between the circle and stem on *d, b* or *p,* and *q.* Letters should sit on the bottom line. Conversely, if the written work is dark and smudgy, with rips or tears, this is a sign of tension and uncertainty, as the child is holding the pencil too tightly, and exerting too much pressure. This could indicate motor control difficulties. Letters, even in primary grades, should be approximately the same size, and the pressure of the pencil on the paper should be uniform.

Watch for a consistent reversal pattern. Does he always reverse *e*'s, and confuse *b, d,* or the stems on *p* and *q*? Watch for reversals on numbers, especially 2, 3, and 5. See if he starts the number 8 at the top or the bottom. In two digit numbers, does he reverse the ten's and one's column?

Does the child organize for work or play? Does he put materials away neatly and on time? Is he ready for recess and lunch time when the other students are ready?

How well can the child move about the room without bumping into or tipping over objects? How well does he handle materials without breaking them (such things as pick-up sticks or jackstraws)?

Can he identify and separate foreground objects from background (near and far away)? Difficulties in differentiating these, especially in pictures, may be an indication of receptive and associative difficulties.

Does he discriminate between sizes and shapes of objects? Can he tell the difference between colors of similar hue, or pick out the smallest article in a group of three or four? Lack of discrimination in these areas could be a clue to associative types of disability.

Can he accomplish a task that requires a sequence of activities? Can he follow directions when the activity involves listening to a series of commands, then carrying these out?

How do objects in space appear to him? Do they stay in place, or do they change place, according to his own body position?

Classroom Tests for M.C.D. Handicaps

Approximately 15 percent of all students in school have some reading disability. While many of these reading problems are due to other causes, as mentioned in Chapter 2, I have found as many as 15 percent of one *class* may be "hidden dyslexics," or may be suffering from minimal cerebral dysfunction handicaps. Several years ago in one of my second grade classes, I discovered four students out of a class of 28 to be dyslexic.

Therefore it seems reasonable to test your entire class via a quick check technique. Then use the results of these as a basis for further testing where suspected disabilities are confirmed.

Since most commercially constructed tests, like the Illinois Test of Psycholinguistic Abilities, are long and involve special preparation, it is best to concentrate on methods a teacher can devise or construct for classroom use. As stated before, most formal behavior assessments must be administered by trained specialists, but there are other ways the classroom teacher can evaluate behavior of students suspected to be dyslexic.

Hearing Comprehension Check. The teacher reads orally from a graded selection, and then a quiz is given on what is heard (reception). The child should be able to understand 70 percent of the material (feedback). You can use selected wordlists, having the child give you the meanings of common words, or you can use stories from basal readers for this test. It can be given individually, and with older children you can use small groups.

Most dyslexics are very bright children, but have a short attention span, and are easily frustrated, especially with their own inability to express themselves.

A dull normal child, or one with a low performance

record, usually will respond more slowly to questions on a quiz. Basically this child usually appears to be calmer, works and speaks more slowly, and will exhibit a slower development rate. While the reactions of the two types may be different, the classroom teacher can employ the same testing methods to discover the basic causes of the reading disability. But along with the testing, remember to *observe* the child on an individual basis, as this will be the heart of your remediation process.

Oral Reading Check. (This can be done with an entire group.) Have each child read two or three sentences aloud, as fast as he can, from the basal reader or another selection. Go to the next child, and proceed in this fashion until all have read. If a child refuses to read, go on to the next one. The teacher tells the child any unknown word, and responds to each child's reading with "good," etc., and moves to the next child. This is a fast survey to check visual reception, and can also be used to check attention span, vocabulary, expression, and comprehension.

Silent Reading Comprehension Check. (This can be done singly or with an entire group or class.) The student reads a two to five page selection, according to grade level. When he finishes, he closes his book and looks at the teacher. (Slow readers can be detected this way.) When all the students in the group have finished, the teacher reads from a prepared sheet of short answer questions and the children write down their answers. They should score at least 70 percent in comprehension. This test is devised to evaluate reception, association and feedback skills.

Auditory Skills (Sound blending). The student should be able to blend analyzed sound components into a unified word whole, then blend them into meaningful sounds. This test can be given individually, but can also be administered to small groups or to an entire class at upper elementary levels, and is designed to check both reception and feedback. Start with two letter words, allowing about two sounds per second. Then work up to longer words. Begin with words like "a-t," "m-e," "o-n," "i-t," pronouncing each vowel and consonant sound distinctly.

Then go to longer words, like "c-a-t," "b-r-a-n," "c-e-n-t-e-r." Don't let the student see your lips as you dictate the list. If they depend on visual cues, they would be able to guess the words. You are after *sound* cues, checking auditory perception.

Visual Memory. When testing in this area, there is no gradation involved. The test just screens out the children with visual problems which might interfere with reception and feedback skills.

Make nonsense word cards from the list given in Chapter 4. Flash these for five seconds. The child must reproduce what he sees on paper. Visual discrimination errors you might spot are:

1. Orientational confusion   (b for p)
2. Structural details   (n for h)
3. Combination of the two   (p for q)

These are reversal type errors. The child who consistently reverses letters should be scheduled for further testing by a specialist.

Visual sequencing. This is the ability to organize visual stimuli in correct spatial order. This involves left to right order. Testing in primary grades is best done individually. Present pictures (line drawings) of a series of objects that would "go together," such as eating utensils, plate, cup, fork, spoon etc., with one or two objects missing from the group. Have the student tell you what is missing. For example in the afore-mentioned list, the saucer could be added and the table knife. The child should be able to tell you these items. Use form boards or the TRY[2] materials presenting a pattern, and show for five seconds, then remove or shuffle the objects and have the child arrange them in proper order. This test will indicate problems in association or imperfect visual closure as well as sequencing ability. For older children, flash a series of numbers

---

[2]George Manolakes and others, *TRY Experiences for Young Children* (67 Irving Place, New York, New York 10013, 1967).

(three or four, according to grade level). Then have the students write down the numbers in the order presented.

No spelling words should be involved in the testing. The child will try to put the letters in order the way he remembers them, rather than concentrate on what is shown, thus causing interference. Use numbers, designs, or simple stick figures for the child to reproduce the sequence. Gradually increase the number of objects or number cards to check length of the visual memory pattern. This test involves both the receptive and feedback operations. Once the testing is finished, this is also an excellent way to train and reinforce the child's visual sequential memory skill.

Motor Skills Check. Have the child identify common objects and tell about them or demonstrate their use. For instance, give him a toy hammer. Watch how he holds it and what movements he makes with it.

Watch the student during sorting, cutting, and pasting activities. Give matching activities which are progressively sequenced in levels of ability. Ask the student to copy a design by putting blocks or pegs together. Jigsaw puzzles are excellent activities for upper elementary grades.

When assuming the child's abilities, remember that association must take place within all sensory areas. That is, there must be a fusion between auditory and visual stimuli. The child matches a sensory image with a motor movement. *How* he performs gives the observer hints of M.C.D. handicaps.

Ways to Help Dyslexic Children

Reading requires an intact perceptual apparatus. The beginning stages of reading depend almost entirely on visual perceptual clues. In later developmental stages, the need for configuration clues decreases a little in importance. As children get older, they will depend on linguistic or conceptual cues. This is one reason why early diagnosis and treatment is so important to reading skills. Since most of the early stages involve basic sight words, if the student cannot perceive these properly he is off to a poor start in reading.

The exercises and techniques given here are beneficial to all elementary school children, but are especially designed to help children with visual perceptual problems which might interfere with reading achievement.

Room atmosphere is important. The room should be bright and cheerful, but visual distractions should be kept at a minimum. If possible, the student should have a quiet place to work, away from other children when frustrations and pressures become more than he can manage, or when you are working alone with him on visual perceptual training. Study carrels (individually enclosed work spaces—usually a desk with raised sides and front which act as a screen) fill this need well.

Also, a "Quiet Corner" is advisable. A student can go here when he wants to be by himself, to read or study in comfort. In my classroom, I utilize several study carrels, and also have my quiet corner where students may go to read or work in quiet. This corner (primary grade) is equipped with a carpet, large floor pillows, a bench along one wall, and a child-sized rocking chair. All my students love it.

Windows prove a great distraction for dyslexic children in a classroom because their attention span is short. Windows at eye level should be kept closed wherever possible, with ventilation and light sources coming from the top sections above the eye level of the child.

Most of the games and activities mentioned in Chapter 5 are applicable to the dyslexic child and should be utilized. Use many and varied lessons to keep the child interested and to keep the frustration level at a minimum. Use activities that will insure success. Involve the whole class or a group within the class, incorporating other students, so the child with M.C.D. problems doesn't feel "different." Most students profit from the exercises, and in most cases feel sympathetic and want to help others, especially in the lower grades.

Some materials I have found helpful are the workbook exercises in the Michigan Tracking Programs written by Dr.

Robert Geake[3] and Dr. Donald E.P. Smith[4] (see Figures 6-1, 6-2).

The Frostig program of developmental workbooks, *Pictures and Patterns*[5] are also very good materials for classroom use. There are three levels of workbooks, so that the child can make continuous progress. The Geake-Smith materials are recommended from primary grades through adult training.

Other ways to help students with M.C.D. dysfunctions are with games. The license plate game, "Keep Away" words, nonsense word drill cards (flashcards), What's Missing, and Merry Mixup are all excellent activities. You will find directions for these in Chapter 10.

Large motor training gives a child a sense of power over his own body, which is very important psychologically. Body control is especially important for a dyslexic child, so plan activities that enhance use of body parts. All activities should be planned to insure success. Start with simple exercises that each child in your classroom can perform; jumping in and out of old automobile tires is excellent, and it particularly appeals to boys because they've seen professional football players doing it on T.V. (Tires can be obtained at little or no expense, if you explain to the wrecking yard dealer your purpose. Most are sympathetic to schools and their lack of equipment.)

Stegel[6] equipment (indoor primary P.E. fixtures) or outdoor gym bars also provide good motor training. Children like to walk with their hands on the overhead ladder or parallel bars. Utilize all P.E. equipment that is available to you. Balance beams can be constructed very simply from 4X4's, 12 feet

---

[3]R. Robert Geake and Donald E.P. Smith, *Visual Tracking* (Ann Arbor, Michigan: Ann Arbor Publishers, 1962).

[4]Donald E.P. Smith and Judith M. Smith, *Word Tracking* (Ann Arbor, Michigan: Ann Arbor Publishers, 1967).

[5]Marianne Frostig, *Developmental Program in Visual Perception* (Chicago: Follett Educational Corp., 1966).

[6]Reproduced by permission of Orinda Union School District, Orinda, California

a b c d e f g h i j k l m n o p q r s t u v w x y z.

Fgn acog zbof hdmi nush pow
tryp kif nurc shd. Mo jins pem ruk.
Rolb nsb ofn lijs buw rog sav. Nry
hnuw wops riz lorn somt. Pojs yut
zak robt tor slaw euqur. Gabl er
cag jefe sem uf nate boxr. Bugp ut
cit que kicb ridg. Wab svz gfu wxyz.

Belj nit loca poku wecf. Hnb ab.
Hirj civer liep kibe miw soge fax.
Cin Soc regl fi bey zod. Ghu plke op.

Min_____Sec_____

Neoz wtvx lky njt sjo uz aetr btc.
gohn wrmz kd eofr. Jho vqr yx vop lm.
Apf oon bcg. Pph ooq wca. Xzt ltoi.

Dojn Xzt kru w ol. Sma bbqo.
doc bn wrar ogf tpu. Dec bgh ih cf. Ya
dfe kcq tw gff. Bjf rb cff. Djc tvd.
Pok sjdf kgect nja bu ceh. Lwnv heg
rnwq kirx pf. Njaf rrxe qeb yne ponaz.

Min_____Sec_____

Figure 6-1

Sample page from *Visual Tracking.* The student is to look
along the row, left to right, and find the first "a" on the line;
then the first "b," the first "c," and so on throughout the
alphabetical sequence embedded in the "words." He cannot
backtrack. When letters are found in proper sequence, the
alphabet can be completed in the exercise.

Reproduced by special permission of R. Robert Geake and
Donald E.P. Smith, *Visual Tracking* (Ann Arbor, Michigan:
Ann Arbor Publishers, 1962), p. 1.

1. The man walked.

She This The Them
me may mad man
talked waked walked walled

2. Joe ran here.

Jim Joe John Jack
run ray ran ram
there then head here

3. Dad is big.

Day Dad Dab Dog
it at as is
bag bug big bog

4. Boys play ball.

Bugs Bays Buys Boys
plan play park page
bill pull ball balk

5. I saw birds.

A I It As
was say way saw
bids birds burst birch

Min _____ Sec _____ .

Fill in:

Boys _____ ball.

Joe _____ here.

The man _____ .

_____ saw birds.

Dad is _____ .

Figure 6-2

Sample page from *Word Tracking.* The student looks at the sentence in bold face type. Then he scans the sentences directly below. He finds the first word on the first line and circles it, the second word on the second line, etc., completing the sequence. Follow-up exercises are given at the bottom of the page. Sentences in the book get progressively longer and more difficult to strengthen sequencing patterns.

Reproduced by special permission of Donald E.P. Smith and Judith M. Smith, *Word Tracking* (Ann Arbor, Michigan: Ann Arbor Publishers, 1967), p. 1.

long. Also, rocking boards, two feet square, balanced (nailed together for safety's sake) on a 6 X 6 X 3 inch block make excellent exercise equipment. (Teachers themselves should be careful on rocking boards, and use a chair as a support. Most teachers also have difficulty with balance!)

Many times, these materials can be donated and constructed by parents. For instance, Stegel equipment can be constructed for less than $200. If this cost is spread over a parent group or P.T.A., it becomes minimal, and the equipment can be used for P.E. activities for the entire school. (Figure 6-3.)

Most of the games, activities, and exercises given here and in Chapter 10 are conducive to entire class activities. Be sure to incorporate large and small muscle activities via your music program and arts and crafts activities. The latter two areas are a very important part of the school curriculum and should not be neglected. Correlating these into your program for children with perceptual disabilities cannot be overemphasized. Moreover, these benefit your entire class, so that all students will become more adept in body control.

PERCEPTUAL DISORDERS AND SOME REMEDIATION TECHNIQUES

Disability Area	Dysfunction	Remediation
Visual Reception	Inability to understand picture or symbol, and to form concepts (to "make sense of what you see").	Sorting tasks, such as color matching of beads, blocks, etc. Have student describe and interpret picture; use of maps, charts, etc. employing much verbalization. "Complete the picture activities (see Chapter 10).
Visual Sequential Memory	Inability to remember a series of symbols; numbers, letters, etc.	Dot-to-dot activities, bead stringing, or like sequential activities.

Disability Area	Dysfunction	Remediation
		Games like "Telephone" or "What's Missing?" *Any* game or handcraft that emphasizes patterning.
Visual Association	Inability to understand visual relationships.	Sorting activities, categorizing, matching games, completion activities, "Complete the Sentence; Story; Paragraph" etc.
Visual Closure	Inability to form a visual whole from parts presented. Inability to distinguish between foreground and background.	Play "What's Missing?" Use Complete the Picture and embedded forms. Pick out all items of same form or type from background of other items.
Auditory Reception	Inability to understand spoken language. Unable to listen, to form imagery. Impaired vocabulary. Information-gathering skills poor.	Question and answer games, games which employ clues, following verbal directions. (Mother, May I and Simon Says). Show and Tell, music and singing games.
Auditory Sequential Memory	Inability to remember more than one auditory direction at a time, or the inability to hear spoken symbols in sequence, e.g., a number sequence such as 3, 2, 4, 1, 6. Child cannot reproduce series vocally.	Use of tape-recorded sequential stories. Games of opposites, finding word relationships, "add-on" games, such as Grocery Store, or any other where they must *listen* to a series of objects, or to a series of commands and carry them out. Repetition games.

Disability Area	Dysfunction	Remediation
Auditory Association	Inability to relate words meaningfully. Unable to make verbal comments of a more automatic sort.	Use of verbal analogies, association games, games of opposites. Finding differences, or the "one that doesn't belong." Comparing, sounds and beats in music. Commercial games such as "Password" and "Concentration."
Auditory Closure	Inability to form a whole auditory gestalt from sounds heard separately. Inability to vocalize whole word from the parts given.	Drill letter sounds. Listening for certain sounds in words. Synthesizing words from parts given. Analyzing word parts. Drill consonant sounds in medial and final position. Listening exercises in general.
Motor Control	Clumsiness; inability to control body movements to student's own satisfaction. Lack of hand-eye coordination.	Role playing games, Charades, plays; coordination exercises on the Stegel; walking a balance beam. Rhythm games and songs, marching to music. Handcrafts. *Any* activity that employs all the sensory modes possible.

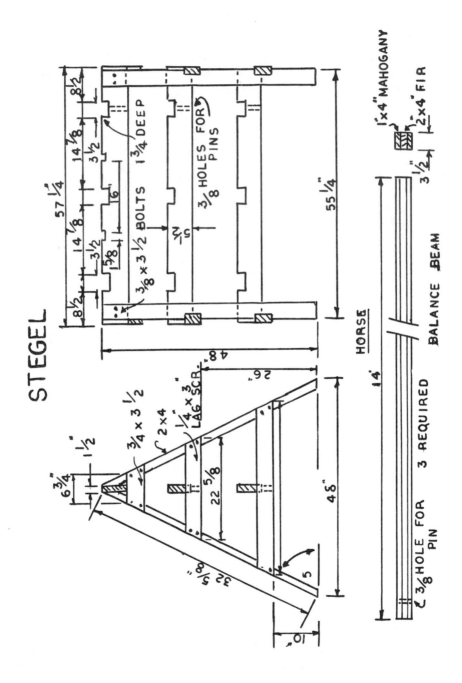

STEGEL

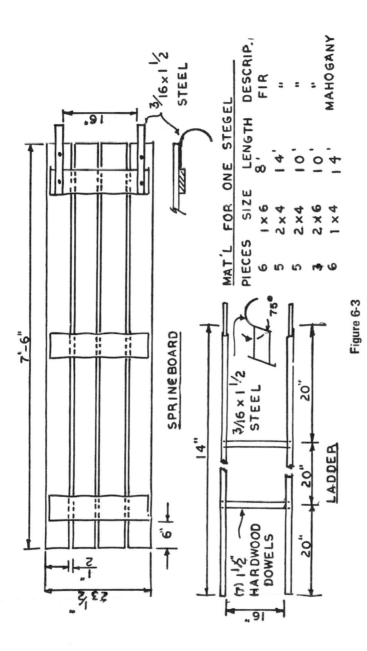

MAT'L FOR ONE STEGEL			
PIECES	SIZE	LENGTH	DESCRIP.
6	1×6	8'	FIR
5	2×4	14'	"
5	2×4	10'	"
3	2×6	10'	"
6	1×4	14'	MAHOGANY

Figure 6-3

Plans for a STEGEL (physical education equipment). Stegel is designed so that it can be assembled and dismantled by students and can be used indoors with mats, or outdoors on grassy areas.

Plans reproduced by permission of Orinda Union School District, Orinda, California.

7

Individual Tests and Testing Techniques
That Bring Remediation in Reading

This chapter is concerned with tests and techniques for determining reading skills, and will delineate types and uses. Five basic types of tests will be discussed: I.Q., perception, readiness, reading, and achievement. They measure the child's learning ability, mental growth, and capacity in reading.

Within each of the five general areas, I will explain the nature of the tests, how and when they are given, and how to use the results in your program. At the end of the chapter there will be a list of some of the tests published for each category, along with comments on their strengths and weaknesses.

A teacher is more than a casual experience to the children of her class. From the time the child enters her class he is in her care. There can be nothing casual or insignificant about the association. I believe that the really dedicated teacher views each student as if the child's whole future depends on what that teacher does in the time allowed.

There is no room for chance in the remediation of reading problems. Like surgery, the teacher cannot afford to guess. Diagnosis is mandatory and the best tools and techniques must be applied because the time is short.

Four Reasons for Testing

There are four basic reasons for testing in your remedial program.

(1) Test to diagnose areas of weakness. This is to save time, so you will not reteach areas in which the student is already competent. By finding which skills need to be retaught you can concentrate on the categories of greatest need.

(2) You must put a floor under the student. That is, you must find out exactly how far *back* to go in individual remediation. In some cases, you must return to pre-reading skills and basic phonics. (A discussion of basic phonics is included in Chapter 3.)

(3) Testing helps evaluate the effectiveness of your program. Keep in mind that not all children learn by the same technique. By evaluating each child's test results you can determine by which method he best learns—visual or auditory, verbal or non-verbal—and can devise an individual plan to present the concepts so he understands and learns best according to his particular abilities. If a child doesn't understand the concept, it may have to be presented in a different way or perhaps *several* ways. (Chapter 5 has a more complete explanation of how children learn through perceptual channels.)

(4) Testing is a good method of establishing objectives for the teacher and her students. Efforts at learning are then directed at correcting each child's particular disability. The goals set must be reasonable, so that they can be met.

Tests should be considered as general *indicators* of student capacities in different curriculum areas, including reading disability. The findings should be used to reinforce teacher observations and to give clues as to the major areas of concern. In a progressive individualized program, testing is a "must."

The Five Types of Tests (Standardized Tests)

I.Q. Tests

Intelligence tests are given to determine how much a child can learn compared to other children of normal ability. They are an indicator of a child's capacity to think and solve problems. From the data attained the teacher can predict the rate of progress for her pupils. By use of I.Q. tests she can also determine whether a child's reading disability is due to a specific deficiency or to just generally low ability.

If a child's scores fall within a certain range (e.g. 90-110) we can expect that child to be *able* to learn at about the same rate as the other children in the classroom. If he falls below this range, he may be a dull-normal child that will progress at a slower rate, or a normal child with a reading disability. I.Q. is tested since we need an indicator of how much growth to expect, and this characteristic governs the *rate* of pupil progress.

In testing children in primary grades, the I.Q. tests given are verbal, using only pictorial type items. This enables a child who cannot read well to still perform satisfactorily on the tests.

In the upper grades, both verbal and non-verbal batteries are provided. The non-verbal items may be either pictorial or numerical. In using a non-verbal battery, prediction of school achievement will be less valid than the verbal battery, as no actual reading-thinking skills are involved. However, it will give an estimate of scholastic aptitude which is not influenced by reading ability. In fact, if a wide discrepancy is noted, it is often an indicator of reading disability. (See page 103.)

Perception Tests

Perception is an important agent in reading disability. Perception tests are designed to determine how a child perceives or "sees" himself and the world about him. Some children are not aware of the different *parts* of their bodies, how they are interconnected, and how they should function. Their motor control is poor, as is their concept of spatial relationships.

Perception tests show the areas of perceptual handicaps; with this type disability, the related visual-motor coordination problems must be treated, along with the remediation in reading, since both factors interact, a situation of cause and effect.

The Frostig Developmental Test of Visual Perception[1] is broken into five subtests: Eye-Motor Coordination, Figure-Ground, Constancy of Shape, Position in Space, and Spatial Relationships. These were devised specifically to discover visual perceptual handicaps in young children, ages three to nine. The test loses validity *after third grade level.* (See page 104.)

The Illinois Test of Psycholinguistic Abilities[2] tests for

---

[1] Marianne Frostig and others, *Developmental Test of Visual Perception* (577 College Ave., Palo Alto, California: Consulting Psychologists Press, 1961).

[2] Samuel A. Kirk and Winifred D. Kirk, *Illinois Test of Psycholinguistic Abilities* (Urbana, Illinois: University of Illinois Press, 1961).

Figure 7-1

On this page, the student has consistently made reversal-type errors (see 1,4,5) which suggest either a perceptual problem, or difficulty in left-to-right orientation. Follow-up and reteaching in this area are indicated.

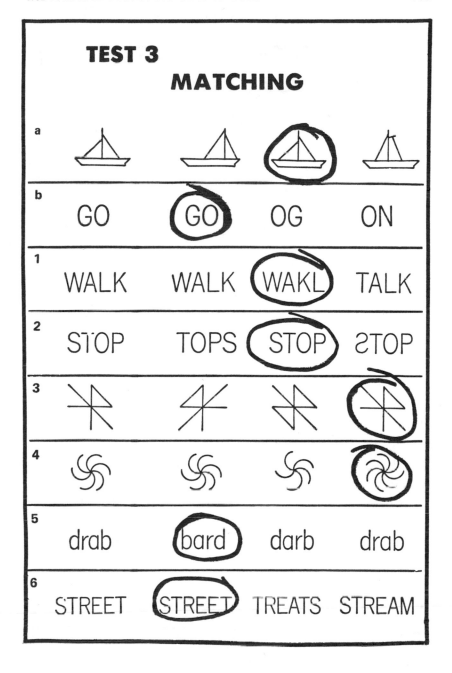

DEVELOPMENTAL TEST
OF VISUAL PERCEPTION

IIa

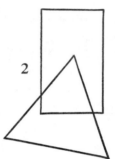
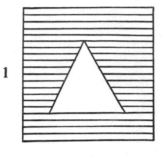
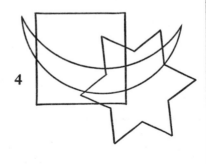

both auditory and visual perceptual handicaps, and is one of the best tests available in this area. Its age range is from three to 12 years. However, the author advises that this test should *not* be given by the classroom teacher unless she has had the specific training necessary for proper administration. Most school districts have this test given by the school psychologist or a trained psychometrist. It is lengthy, has 12 categories, and the classroom teacher may not have time to administer, score, and analyze the test. If auditory and visual perceptual problems are suspected, it is best to have the I.T.P.A. test given by a school specialist. (See page 107.)

Ruth was referred to me by her classroom teacher. She seemed to be always playing, rather than attending to assignments. When the teacher gave Ruth specific instructions, the child would complete only the first part of the assignment. She never finished her work without three or four reminders.

On testing with the Illinois Test of Psycholinguistic Abilities, we discovered that Ruth had a severe auditory sequential memory deficit. That is, she could not remember a series of instructions given orally. She could hear only the first command; the second, third, etc., in the series were "blotted out" and not heard by the child.

Proper remediation for this deficit consisted of giving Ruth

Figure 7-2

Sample page from the Developmental Test of Visual Perception, Test II a. The child is shown cards having one shape, such as a triangle or rectangle. Then on his booklet he must outline the shape from the embedded figures shown. He is penalized for lifting his crayon, or if the outline of the figure is interrupted.

only one oral command at a time, at the start. Then, when she could successfully complete the assignment for several lessons, the teacher increased the commands by giving two of them. Gradually, with teacher and student working together, Ruth's handicap was overcome, and she could follow a series of oral commands, and complete them in proper order.

Readiness Tests

Readiness tests are usually given at the end of kindergarten or beginning first grade, before actual teaching is begun. Readiness testing before beginning reading instruction appraises the child's pre-reading skills. (The complete list of pre-reading skills is given in Chapter 2.) A good readiness test should evaluate visual discrimination, analogies and relationships, knowledge of letter names and letter sounds, and motor control. Most of the recently published tests include a subtest for visual perception, which, as stated earlier, is an important factor in predicting reading success.

Readiness also refers to progress at each *grade* level, and can be measured by use of the readiness tests which accompany the basal readers. Is the child ready to begin reading instruction in the readers at his particular grade level? Use of these test results will indicate where the student needs more instruction in the skills areas, and what skills he has already mastered.

Should a child score particularly low on a readiness test, he should not be excluded from the reading program. The test

Figure 7-3

Profile of abilities from protocol (test booklet) of the Illinois Test of Psycholinguistic Abilities. The profile indicates a severe auditory sequential memory deficit.

Reproduced from the test protocol, Illinois Test of Psycholinguistic Abilities, Revised Edition, by Samuel A. Kirk, James J. McCarthy, and Winifred D. Kirk, University of Illinois Press, Urbana, Illinois 61801, 1968.

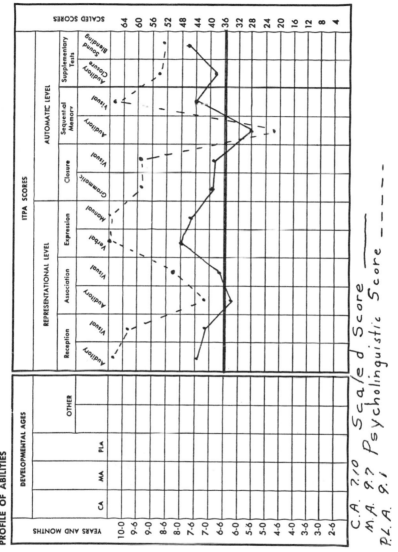

findings should be utilized to help reteach or reinforce skills areas needed to insure success in beginning reading instruction for the youngster.

Readiness tests are given to obtain information about a student's perceptual and cognitive development and they show the amount of prior training and experience of each child. By observation during readiness testing, the teacher can estimate attention span, emotional maturity, language background, health, and motor coordination—all pertinent to the child's beginning reading instructional program.

The Metropolitan Readiness Test[3] is broken into six areas: word meaning, listening, matching, alphabet, numbers, and

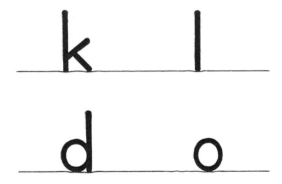

Figure 7-4

Sample from the Gates, MacGinitie Readiness Test (Test VI, Visual Motor Coordination). After explicit instructions from the teacher, the child completes the letter on the right following the model given on the left.

Reprinted by permission of the publisher from Gates— MacGinitie Reading Tests, Readiness Skills. (New York: Teachers College Press, copyright © 1969 by Teachers College, Columbia University).

---

[3]Gertrude H. Hildreth and others, *Metropolitan Readiness Tests* (New York: Harcourt, Brace, Jovanovich, Inc., 1964).

copying. By looking at raw scores (number correct in each subtest) you can make an estimate of the child's ability in that area. However, your basis for judging whether the child is ready for more formal reading instruction should be based on the total score, percentile rank, and letter rating. (See page 102.)

The Gates-MacGinitie Readiness Test[4] has seven categories: listening comprehension, auditory discrimination, visual discrimination, following directions, letter recognition, visual-motor coordination, and auditory blending. The addition of the test in visual-motor coordination is useful in finding students with perceptual problems. It corresponds somewhat to the copying subtest on the Metropolitan Readiness Test. These two are good commercially published tests to help in primary grades. There is a more complete list of readiness tests given at the end of the chapter.

Comprehension Test III

Directions: Read each story and the sentences under the story. Put an "X" in the box in front of the right answer for each sentence.

A.   Betsy has a new pet. It is brown with a white tail. She wanted to give it something to eat. But she couldn't find a bone.

Figure 7-5

This paragraph is from Comprehension Test III, MASTERY TEST TO ACCOMPANY SHINING BRIDGES, by Edward R. Sipay.

Reproduced by special permission of The MacMillan Company, A CCM COMPANY. Copyright © 1968), New York, New York 10022.

---

[4]Arthur I. Gates and Walter H. MacGinitie, Readiness Skills (Teachers College, Columbia University, New York: Teachers College Press, 1968).

Reading Tests

Reading tests are used to locate areas of weakness and to verify a hypothesis concerning a child's reading ability. The instruments are divided into subtests pertaining to different reading skills, and it is these subtests with which we are concerned, as they will show exact places of need.

Reading tests help put the "floor" under the student. By looking at the examples of reading tests given at the end of this chapter, you will see that the subheadings divide the skills into different categories. The most common categories are vocabulary, word attack, prefixes and suffixes, compound words, initial and final consonant recognition, medial consonants, vowel sounds, and comprehension.

Reading achievement tests are usually given after a child has mastered the primers and one or two levels of a basal reader series. These tests should be used as guidelines for teaching the word attack skills and to locate places where reteaching and/or remediation are needed, and are best given in small groups or individually. The testing manuals suggest ten to 15 students to a group, but smaller groups of four or five students each are easier to handle.

Achievement Tests

Achievement surveys cover most of the curriculum areas, and measure what the child has learned. As stated elsewhere, these tests are designed for use with all grade levels, and are usually given district-wide as a comparison against (a) other schools, (b) other districts, (c) state norms, and (d) national norms. They are mentioned here because they do require reading skills. Subtests in reading indicate in what specific area the student may be experiencing difficulty. Reading achievement batteries are usually given to gauge how much of the content and word attack skills have been mastered when the student has completed a level of the basal reader series.

Examples of good tests are those published by Harper and Row.[5]

Achievement tests also may consist of a survey type or *battery* of tests given to appraise academic progress in *all* curriculum areas, and show a student's strengths and weaknesses in each subject matter area. The subtests from this battery can also be used as a basis for remedial reading diagnosis since they require reading ability, and ever-increasing skill in reading is basic to progress through the grades. This latter type is usually given throughout a district at successive grade levels to compare against state or national norms.

Guide to Commercially-Published Tests

The best guide to commercially published tests is Oskar K. Buros' Mental Measurements Yearbook.[6] This volume, which is periodically revised and updated, gives a complete list of all tests in each curricular area, plus a review of each test, what it measures and how it is used, and compares it to others in the field. The yearbook is usually found in the Teachers' Professional Library in every school district, and is a handy reference for all curricular areas.

The tests for reading are broken into categories according to skills areas, such as readiness, comprehension, word attack skills, etc., and are also compiled by academic level: elementary, junior high, high school, and university or college level. There is also a separate volume which contains only reading tests.[7] (Some of the better tests are listed at the end of this chapter.)

---

[5]Harper and Rowe, Publishers, Inc., School Dept., 2500 Crawford Ave., Evanston, Illinois 60201.

[6]Oskar K. Buros, *Mental Measurements Yearbook*, (7th edition), (Highland Park, New Jersey: Gryphon Press, 1972).

[7]Oskar K. Buros, *Reading Tests and Reviews* (Highland Park, New Jersey: Gryphon Press, 1968).

How to Choose the Type of Test You Need

Before testing, the teacher usually has some idea of where an individual child is having difficulty. She may have gathered this information from personal observation, cumulative records, last year's teachers, or conferences with parents. Telltale clues manifest themselves in the actual reading process, in attitudes and behavior and in other subject matter areas, especially social studies and the language arts. If a child cannot read the grade level texts in these areas, it will be evidenced by both his oral reading and his written work.

There are three steps in choosing the test to fit the needs of an individual student.

A good way to begin is by giving a readiness (placement-type) test for your grade level to the whole class. If there is none available to accompany your basal reader, use the final achievement test for the previous year. Using this type of test will not only help in diagnosing the individual student with whom you are concerned, but will catch all children with disabilities, especially a too quiet child, or the one who covers up. In addition, the over-all testing will indicate weak areas among students, areas which can be taught to the whole group needing those particular skills.

While testing, consider the following questions: Does the student have the visual discrimination necessary to understanding what the letters on a printed page mean? Can he make analogies and relationships? Does he have the motor control and the hand-eye coordination necessary for seeing and interpreting the words in a book?

Next, set up a check list for each student. There is an excellent one given in DeChant[8], or you can set up your own. This, along with your personal observation and oral reading

---

[8]Emerald DeChant, *Diagnosis and Remediation of Reading Disability* (West Nyack, New York: Parker Publishing Company, Inc., 1968), pp. 31-32, 39.

tests, will give you a starting point. An oral check list is helpful in discovering what kinds of errors are made. (There are many commercial oral reading tests given in the list at the end of this chapter.) Check lists usually accompany the test manuals, or are listed on the front of the evaluation sheet.

Finally, list on the check sheet or on file cards the areas you feel need the remediation most critically. Study the subtests on each student, using them to verify your preliminary findings and classroom observations. By recording and analyzing data, you can find areas in which you can group two or three children with similar handicaps together, to save time.

If a child wanders, talks to neighbors, or says he's finished and you discover his work is of poor caliber or incomplete, then in most cases this child is not functioning on his proper reading level.

On occasion, I have found "sleepers" ("good talkers," if you will.) These children were very verbal, had good backgrounds in subject matter, could discuss topics and think originally and creatively, but lacked basic skills in both reading and writing. By watching behavior, I suspected that they had a disability, and began testing. Diagnosis and remediation followed. Teacher judgment and classroom observation are still the best ways to find and diagnose areas of weakness.

Recording Data from Published Tests

When you have completed your testing, results should be recorded in the test booklet in the spaces provided, and also on a separate class record sheet. The pupil form is usually printed on the front of the test booklet. After you have recorded and analyzed the data, the test booklet itself can be discarded, and the front cover inserted into the student's cumulative folder.

The class record sheet is used to record scores for the entire class. By studying this sheet, you can obtain an over-all picture of the class and make general comparisons as to where the students are having difficulty, and where regrouping might be necessary to reinforce a skill. These class record sheets are also convenient for evaluating your teaching methods. You can see at a glance where the entire class might be deficient in one category, and this should initiate a change in your reading program.

One of the best ways to record data is by use of a line graph. The teacher can readily see the peaks and depressions indicating a child's strengths and weaknesses.

Don't forget about anecdotal records. These are important and very necessary to evaluating your program. They show evidence of rapport, and also bear the tell-tale signs when a child is uneasy or uncomfortable in his reading.

Interpreting Test Results for Classroom Use

After you have given a test, interpreting or analyzing is best done by means of comparison. I usually test three to five students at a time. With older children, at intermediate level, it is possible to test an entire class. I find it easier to mark and score one subtest or section at a time and record it on the space provided on the test booklet. Most reading test booklets have a dotted line printed across the recording sheet to show age and grade norms for that particular test level. By marking the score right away, you can tell if the student is above or below the norm for that particular subtest, and thus see where he might be having difficulty. Also, by scoring several tests at a time, you can compare one student's score to others, as a criteria for placement, and as a further help in setting up an individual program for him.

When analyzing, compare each child's raw score to the norms given in the manual. Take one area at a time and check scores against the norms for his age or grade. If his scores fall below the mean or norm, then he is obviously experiencing difficulty and will need remediation or reteaching in the area indicated by the subtest. As an example, one of the first tests given in a test booklet for any grade level is sight vocabulary. If a child misses over half the examples, then he will need to learn basic sight vocabulary as the first step in remediation. This child is also deficient in phonics background, so the next step is to introduce the consonant sounds in initial and final position. Remember to move slowly, and insure success at every step. By moving slowly, you can make sure the child learns correctly and thus there will be less reteaching later on.

Utilizing Test Results

Once testing and classroom observations have been completed, you can begin to make individual oral reading checks on the students with suspected difficulties, and you can verify findings by looking at the student's work in the curriculum related areas. During reading time you can continue to test individual students whom you suspect have problems, leaving the other students to work on individualized projects related to their reading assignments.

The child who enters your classroom in the middle of the school year also needs testing for possible problems and to verify academic levels. A reading test is very good evidence of over-all ability in most curriculum areas.

Recently, I discovered a child with severe reading problems by giving a simple applied phonics test. While the rest of my class knew at least part of their consonant and vowel sounds, this youngster, new to our school, had no concept of the separate sounds in spoken words. Therefore, the first step in remediation with this child's individualized program was to teach him phonics.

I have found in my own classroom that my students are very interested in my record cards; and if a child is experiencing difficulty in one area and is *aware* of it, he tends to want to improve. When he sees his own record and his successes are recorded, it proves to be a great motivator. Closer rapport can be established, and the child is then interested in moving to another category to help himself improve.

Keep in mind that children learn from each other, and the small group will feel satisfaction from helping each other and working together. These children also enjoy being "teacher." In my own classroom they love to show or explain something they have learned to another child who is having the same difficulty. Many times I will hear, "Teacher, I know how to do that. May I help her?" This is another way to let the child have success, another way to motivate.

Children *know* when they have problems. If they know you care, and will help them, and are completely honest in showing them their record cards, they are more willing to work with you. Always convey a sincere interest and a positive attitude that you *know* they will succeed. This pat on the back works wonders for a child who is unsure of himself.

Teacher-Made Tests

A standardized test is given to verify areas of weakness, and to compare against other students in class, grade, school, or district level. For new students, or at the beginning of the year, it will provide clues for further investigation of those with reading problems. Teacher-made tests are given to check your conjecture that a child might have a problem, to verify his immediate learnings, and to see where further drill or teaching is needed.

The purpose of teacher-made tests is to check the child's mastery level, and to determine where remediation begins. The teacher also tests to check progress in her program. Since she is working at individual levels, she may be using many different types of materials. Her tests must correspond with the materials she is using in her classroom. In other words, her tests should correlate with flashcards, books, games, etc. that are utilized in her program. For example, if she has cut a story from an old reader or typed out a story, the comprehensive questions would cover the material used. The sight vocabulary should include words taken from the story, and word attack and phonics drills should be included. Special care should be given to vocabulary development to ensure the child knows the *meaning* of each word. Many times he can "sound out" the word but doesn't know what it means, nor can he pick up the meaning from context clues.

Always make sure the selections used match the child's *maturity* level. A child having reading difficulties in sixth grade is not interested in "Run, Dick, run!" He is interested in cars, space, sports, etc. Teachers should look for high interest-low vocabulary materials to implement their program. There are many of these series published especially for the less able student. The Checkered Flag Series for upper grades, and the Dan Frontier Series for primary level students are published especially for boys. There are also high interest-low vocabulary series about animals, true-life adventures, forest rangers, mysteries, and so on, to motivate even the most reluctant reader. A list of these types of readers and their publishers is given in Chapter 12.

Oral Reading Spot Check Techniques

Many children will look at the print on a page without actually reading the sentences and understanding the meaning. They are "word callers." They can sound out the words but don't understand the content of the story or paragraph. One good way to check oral reading is to cut up old readers. Take a story from the reader and make two copies—one for the student and one for you to mark errors. Have the child read out loud, while you mark your copy showing the mistakes he makes. When the child has finished reading, analyze the mistakes and transfer the information to the student record card or check sheet. By finding the number and kinds of mistakes, you can decide which area to remediate first. (See page 118.)

While preparing the test sheets, a set of questions to go with the story can be devised as a comprehension check. A good method is to write a question for each sentence in the story.

When the child finishes reading the story, you then have the questions to determine if the child understood what he read, and to check vocabulary. (Also, with these stories, or similar ones, you can later use a line-by-line reading approach to teach the child how to find answers to questions. He will learn to look for "what the sentence has to say.")

ORAL READING TEST

Little Bunny was in the yard.
He was in the yard to play.
He had fun in the yard.
Teeny and Weeny ran after Bunny.
Buster ran after Teeny and Weeny
to make them go away.

Don ran to Teeny and Weeny.
"You cannot get Bunny," he said.[9]

Figure 7-6

On this sample page words are marked as on the teacher's copy to show which types of errors the child makes. Note reversal of "saw" for "was." A check above a word indicates it was unknown. Substitution is noted as "sub."

This type of comprehension check is also a very good technique to teach silent reading because the child is encouraged to find the answer. From this beginning the student is guided toward writing short answers, especially in the upper grades, as proof that he understands the reading. If he has great difficulty putting answers on paper, you can have him write the first two or three words of the sentence that proves the answer to be correct, and then cite the page and paragraph number. Children like to prove their answers in upper grades, so this method has proven very effective for poor writers.

---

[9]William H. Burton and others, *Our Happy Ways* (Indianapolis, Indiana: Bobbs-Merril Co., 1955).

A child's creative writing ability is often a measure of his reading ability. If he has difficulty putting anything on paper, be suspicious. The child may say, "I don't know what to write." Lots of encouragement is needed to get such a student to put *anything* down on paper. The teacher should try to persuade the child to write at least one sentence on his paper. If you can get him to write one sentence, both you and he have experienced success, and next time, maybe he will be able to write two. The beauty of individualizing instruction is that the teacher can modify her lessons to fit each child's capabilities. If a child actually can't write but one sentence and only think of one fact, any attempt to force him to do more, especially in the early stages of your remedial program, can only frustrate his efforts and defeat your purpose.

Low Sight Vocabulary Techniques

A good way to find children with vocabulary problems is with the spelling lesson. For testing of spelling and phonics ability there are several effective techniques.

Find or make a vocabulary list of representative words for the student's grade level, and the grades below. Remember that spelling texts lag one year behind the developmental reading level. The vocabulary used in a basal reader for third grade will not be presented for spelling mastery until fourth grade. If the child misses 25 to 50 percent of the words on the grade level list, the material is too difficult. Drop back one level and repeat the procedure. Keep dropping back by grade level until the student can spell 95 percent of the words on your test sheet. This will be his developmental spelling level. Vocabulary skills can then begin from this point.

It is a good idea to set up a 70 word check test, comprised of ten words from each grade level, one to seven, to keep handy. Then you will have it to check *all* students in your classroom. These words can be compiled from old spelling texts or from the basal readers.

70 WORD SPELLING TEST

Grade 1	Grade 2	Grade 3	Grade 4
come	bag	above	army
book	cup	dish	autumn
home	fat	funny	honest
with	bed	swim	candle
can	box	sure	busy
look	road	wait	beat
ball	your	window	answer
and	stop	children	cost
his	once	I'm	pumpkin
my	today	Mrs.	together

Grade 5	Grade 6	Grade 7
ache	active	accurate
attack	agent	basketball
English	calendar	encourage
journey	fraction	globe
library	invent	magazine
neighbor	forgotten	license
lump	passage	occurred
saddle	relief	provide
president	twelfth	reasonable
though	unpaid	cabinet

Figure 7-7

If you have just begun your program (early in the year) you can compile a list of words from your current teacher's manual for spelling. The students will not have been exposed to these words as yet, but will already have them in their speaking, reading, and listening vocabulary. Spellers can also be borrowed from other grade levels, so that you can check for vocabulary mastery level.

Another way to test for low sight vocabulary difficulties is to use a graded vocabulary list similar to the one published by Botel[10]. From this list you can select representative words for your grade level and the levels below. If the child misses 25 to 50 percent of the words on the list, the material at that grade level is too difficult.

Phonics Check

One of the best ways to check phonics mastery is to use a "nonsense word" test. This test should be composed of one syllable and two syllable classifications, so that the student must listen to both beginning and ending consonants, and consonants in medial position. Also, with this type of test you can check for short vowel sounds. For example, in the nonsense word "bod," the child would have to identify initial "b" and final "d" for the consonants, and short "o" sound for the vowel. This is an excellent indicator of how well the child hears the separate sounds in spoken words. A detailed list of phonics nonsense words appears in Chapter 4.

Whisper Test for Hearing

When evaluating phonics ability, it is a good idea to make sure the student has adequate hearing. Many times, borderline hearing loss will result in a phonics disability. A whisper test can verify your suspicion of such a loss.

Darken the room slightly, so the student cannot depend on visual clues. Place him at the front of the room, and stand about 20 feet behind him. Whisper several commands for him to follow. If he cannot follow the directions, or doesn't seem to understand, then further testing by the school nurse is indicated.

---

[10]Morton Botel, *Botel Predicting Readability Levels* (Chicago: Follett Publishing Company, 1962).

Silent Reading

Make certain that a student is actually reading the material assigned and is not just looking at the words by using a line-by-line technique. Have him read the line or sentence and then ask him a specific question *about* that line or sentence.

Usually this just involves the teacher turning the sentence around to make the question. If the child cannot give you the answer or explain the material in his own words, he is not reading it, just looking at it (a form of silent word calling).

Repeat the procedure with several sentences from a page or paragraph.

If you do not want to use the basal reader for this, it might be helpful to type the material. Make at least two copies and use double spacing so the type is easily read by the student. With this arrangement the teacher can mark her copy, showing just where the student makes errors. Then she can analyze it later for use in her individualized remedial program.

COMMERCIALLY-PUBLISHED TESTS FOR USE IN CLASSROOM DIAGNOSIS

I.Q. Tests

1. Peabody Picture Vocabulary Test (PPVT), American Guidance Service, Inc., Minneapolis, Minnesota 1959. Ages 3 and up. A series of pictures. Administrator pronounces stimulus word; child picks correct picture from four shown. No reading ability required. Test is short, requiring only 15 minutes. Normed. A good fast test. (Also a good visual perception test.)

2. California Tests of Mental Maturity (CTMM). California Test Bureau, Monterey, California, 1963. Six levels. Measures language and non-language skills. Well-constructed tests, good at all grade levels. Widely used.

3. Lorge Thorndike Intelligence Tests, Houghton Mifflin, Boston, Massachusetts, 1964. Tests for all grade levels. Well-constructed, widely used.

4. SRA Tests of Educational Ability, Science Research Associates, Inc., Chicago, Illinois, 1962. One form, three levels for intermediate and upper grades. Depends heavily on reading skill.

Perception Tests

1. Frostig Developmental Test of Visual Perception, Consulting Psychologists Press, Palo Alto, California, 1964. Predicts learning success. Use to screen for visual or motor disabilities. Ages 5 to 9 only.

2. Illinois Test of Psycholinguistic Abilities, University of Illinois Press, Urbana, Illinois, 1961. Screens for visual, auditory perception, and motor control, ages 2 to 12. To be administered by school psychologist or psychometrist.

3. Screening Test for Identifying Children with Specific Language Disability (Slingerland), Educators Publishing Service, Inc., Cambridge, Massachusetts, 1967, grades 1 to 3. Rather difficult to administer.

Readiness Tests

1. Gates-MacGinitie Reading Tests: Readiness Skills, Teachers College Press, New York, New York, 1968. Tests in nine areas, listening, comprehension, etc. To be administered individually. An excellent test.

2. Lee-Clark Reading Readiness Test, California Test Bureau, Monterey, California, 1943. Three parts, weighted heavily toward visual discrimination of picture forms.

3. Metropolitan Readiness Tests, Harcourt, Brace, Jovanovich, Inc., New York, New York, 1939. Test is a little broader in scope than most. Measures readiness in reading, arithmetic, and writing. Takes longer to give—about 70 minutes. Still widely used and considered very reliable.

4. Murphy-Durrell Reading Readiness Analysis, Harcourt, Brace, Jovanovich, Inc., New York, New York, 1949. Contains a checklist of items; motor, social and emotional factors to predict success in reading.

Diagnostic Reading Tests

1. Botel Reading Inventory, Follett Publishing Co., Chicago, Illinois, 1966. Grades 1-4. Tests cover all levels of reading placement. A good useful informal test.

2. Gates Advanced Primary Reading Tests, Teachers College Press, New York, New York, 1943. Grades 2-3. A good survey test for word recognition, sentence reading and paragraph reading. Administration time, about 50 minutes. Old but still a very reliable test.

3. Gates Basic Reading Tests, Teachers College Press, New York, New York, 1958. Manual suggests grades 3-5, but I feel it is best used with grade 5 and above. Much too difficult for grade 3.

4. McCullough Word Analysis Tests (Experimental Edition), Ginn and Co., Princeton, New Jersey, 1963. Grades 4-6. Stress on word attack skills. A good test. It is well normed.

5. Roswell-Chall Diagnostic Reading Test of Word Analysis Skills, Essay Press, New York, New York, 1959. Grades 2-6. An individual test, mostly phonics. It's a bit brief but gives an informal inventory of the child's needs.

Oral Reading Tests

1. Gilmore Oral Reading Test, Harcourt, Brace, Jovanovich, Inc., New York, New York, 1952. Grades 1-8. Tests pronunciation, comprehension, reading rate. Easy to give; can be administered and scored objectively. A very good test.

2. Gray Oral Reading Test, Bobbs-Merrill C., Inc., Indianapolis, Indiana, 1967. Grades 1 to adult. Tests for seven types of errors: word recognition, mispronunciation, omissions, insertions, substitutions, repetitions, and inversions. This is a very good test.

Achievement Tests

1. American School Achievement Tests (same as California Achievement Tests) California Test Bureau, Monterey, California, 1963. Grades 1-14. A good over-all survey battery, but scores on tests with less than 15 items not considered too reliable. Subtests on reading; word meaning and word recognition pretty short, useful in diagnosis only. Paragraph meaning is a good check on comprehension. This is one of the most recently published test batteries.

2. Cooperative Primary Tests, Educational Testing Service, Inc., Princeton, New Jersey, 1967. Grades 1-3. Test measures word reading, paragraph reading, and comprehension. A good instrument but a bit long. I would suggest at least two separate sessions.

3. Iowa Tests of Basic Skills, Houghton Mifflin, Boston, Massachusetts, 1956. Grades 3-9. Five separate tests: vocabulary, reading, comprehension, language skills, work study skills, arithmetic. Reliability high. Quite long to give, requiring four sessions.

4. Metropolitan Achievement Tests, Harcourt, Brace, Jovanovich, Inc., New York, New York, 1964. Four levels: primary, elementary, inter-

mediate, and advanced. All levels contain vocabulary and reading subtests. Primary and elementary subtests call for quite a bit of reading skill, which makes it a good diagnostic test.

5. Stanford Achievement Tests, Harcourt, Brace, Jovanovich, Inc., New York, New York, 1964. Multi-level tests make this a good device for continuous checking of progress through the grades. High reliability, and considered valid for the old standardized curricula.

READING DISABILITY PROBLEMS AND REMEDIATION

PROBLEM	REMEDIATION
Low sight vocabulary	Use Basic Dolch list, have child memorize words.
Word substitutions: "the" for "and," "but" for "or," etc.	Review of basic small words, flash-cards of small words, oral reading drill, child to find own mistakes when oral reading is completed.
Word repetition ("back track-ing")	Usually due to insecurity. Check basic vocabulary. If student knows all words he should, do lots of oral reading to other students and at home. Weekly oral reading to teacher for five minute periods. Tachistoscopic exercises to encourage left to right orientation. (Cover work as student reads left to right so that he can't "backtrack.")
Word substitution (nouns)	Basic word analysis skills, phonics clues, context clues, use of dictionary markings as clues to pronunciation. Syllabication drill.
Slurring of sounds	Lack of confidence and poor phonics. Drill with basic phonics, pronunciation of basic word lists. Phonics games. Extensive use of tape recorder, so child can hear own voice, can begin to hear and correct his own mistakes.

PROBLEM	*REMEDIATION*
Monotone reader	Tape recorder drill. Work on plays and poetry; plays for getting the "feel" of words, and poetry to aid rhyme and rhythm. Dr. Seuss books are good for this.
Letter and word reversals	Check for perceptual handicap in primary grades. Use left to right orientation drill. Some reversals caused by repetition (see No. 3), causing the child to read backwards. More tachistoscopic exercises. Use of a marker to cover the words already read.
Perceptual-motor	Auditory and kinesthetic exercises. In lower grades Frostig patterning and exercises. Grades 4-5-6, use Fernald techniques; sandpaper tracing of letters, tactile exercises and drill.
Context reading	Usually careless habits, too great a dependency on picture clues. (Child sees "bowl," says "dish." More close reading activities, and oral reading drill. Fill in the blank exercises where student finds exact word from the selection and fills it in.
Mispronunciation or omission of common prefixes and suffixes.	Related to disability above; more close reading, tape recorder drill, so student can spot own errors. Design seatwork exercises emphasizing use of "un," "re," etc.
Medial vowel errors	Poor ear training. Drill on short vowel sounds first, in one syllable words. Use Lippincott approach. Oral-auditory exercises, listening games. Encourage much oral expression.

PROBLEM	*REMEDIATION*
Word Omissions and insertions	Use lots of close reading; design a question to match each sentence in a short reading selection. Child to answer each question orally. Lots of oral drill. Use tape recorder. Have student listen to own taped voice while reading the passage again, then to find own mistakes and point them out to you.

8

Individualized Reading Instruction to Fit Specific Needs

Up to this point we have covered the multitude of problems, symptoms, causes, and techniques unique to reading instruction. At all times we have been writing about individuals and individual difficulties, but simultaneously we have emphasized that the condition which must always be accepted is the membership of the student in a class.

The treatment of individual problems of students in a class of 30 or more is not an unfamiliar situation for a good teacher. It is not the thrust of this chapter to indicate or reveal any earthshaking techniques of teaching, but rather to discuss and enumerate practical, everyday methods which have been tested under the conditions experienced by the average teacher. As my husband is prone to say, quoting from "archy" the poetic cockroach,

... for should i tell my friends i d drink
the hudson river dry
a tidal wave might come and turn
my statements to a lie.[1]

The condition assumed at this point is that of a class of students, each of whom have been tested and categorized according to capability and specific reading problem.

At this point the teacher is faced with the organizational problems of individualizing corrective and progressive instruction for all of his students. If he does it well, he will be able to accomplish his goals without undue stress and with only a few minor calamities. (Let's face it—some things are beyond our control.)

The Basic Goals of Individualization—A General Statement

The goal of the program for your classroom is to provide an atmosphere for self-actualization so each student can learn how to learn! In our era of changing technology, many skills may be needed for an individual to earn a living during his working years because he may have to change jobs several times due to changing technology. Therefore, we need to teach him how to think.

We want a child to enjoy learning and regard it as a challenge, and we must try to develop and broaden his interests at the same time we are building his self-reliance and independence. A child learns to make choices in a non-threatening atmosphere and should feel an acceptance of his decisions by the teacher. He should have a chance to question an authority's statement, and thus learn to exercise his own judgment and so might question the teacher's statements or opinions. After all, teachers are people, and people are fallible.

---

[1]"prudence" from the book *archy and mehitabel* by Don Marquis. Copyright © 1927 by Doubleday & Company, Inc. Reprinted by permission of the publisher.

The child needs to develop self-acceptance concerning his own limitations. He should be encouraged to work to full capacity, but also to accept his own failures, mistakes, and disappointments.

When organizing your individualized approach, keep the basic goals of the *learner* in mind: [2]

1. To help himself, schoolmates, and school to improve.
2. To enjoy school, and to be prompt.
3. To learn to work independently.
4. To choose "smart" things to do as his learning tasks.
5. To accept a disappointment without malice or frustration.
6. To show an interest in new things.
7. To treat others kindly and with understanding.
8. To develop self-discipline.
9. To excel in one or more academic areas.

These goals must not be forgotten in remediation. There is no single approach to individualized instruction; the program must be set up by the teacher to fit *her* needs and capabilities as well as meet the needs of her students.

In most cases when first starting out, it is difficult to know where to begin. Here are some basic questions that must be considered: (1) Does a child have a specific reading problem; if so, what is it? (2) At what level do I need to start instruction? (3) When should I start the program? (4) In what sort of environment should instruction occur? (5) What methods and materials are available and most appropriate for the learning situation? (6) How do I organize my instructional groups? and (7) How do I judge or evaluate whether or not the students are learning?

---

[2] Joyce Fern Glasser, *Elementary School Learning Center for Independent Study* (West Nyack, New York: Parker Publishing Co., Inc., 1971), p. 44.

Four Plans for Individualization

There are four general types of individualized instruction. These are: school determined pacing, self-directed instruction, individualized instruction, and independent study programs.

School determined pacing. In this form of instruction each child is individually diagnosed (prescriptive teaching). Then the school determines what and how the child is to be taught. Under this program the school determines the objectives for the learner, but the child moves at his own pace.

The open classroom concept recognizes that the energy, emotions, attention span, curiosity, and competitive spirit of the children are best utilized by *not* attempting to get some 30 of them to do the same thing at the same time. The differences in capability of fast and slow learners makes the conventional classroom and environment wasteful of time and talent, and one which by its very nature of time limits on activities, prevents individualization.

Self-directed instruction. In this program the child chooses the materials and determines how he wants to proceed. The teacher determines the *structure* of the child's program, and the teacher and school administration set the learning objectives and goals—the basic criteria. The pace and material are then determined by the student.

It is normal for teachers to be a bit apprehensive when first trying open planning because of the need to monitor several different activities at one time. The key to success is the ability to "hang loose." In time, the teacher finds to his great surprise and delight that he has developed perceptual talents which bring order out of apparent chaos.

He will also find that he has help from an unexpected source, the children themselves. Children like to work together and are generous about helping each other.

Individualized instruction. Under this program, the student sets his own learning goals, but once these goals are chosen, the student follows a program set up by the teacher and must use specific materials selected by the school. The student works at his own speed, but the teacher is there to provide assistance or guidance. He also monitors progress and provides the motivation required to insure satisfactory improvement. The teacher's methods require subtlety, for the child must be given incentive and direction while remaining unaware of the "push."

This program is most often seen in high school programs where students use Learning Activity Packets (LAPS), as certain curriculum requirements must be met to receive credit and their high school diploma.

Independent study program. Under this method, the learner establishes his own learning objectives and the method by which he will achieve them. In most cases, only students with exceedingly high academic potential are capable of this type of program.

Self-directed instruction and independent study are both designed for children of high learning potential and a well-developed degree of maturity. Individualized instruction is designed for children of all learning capabilities and can be utilized at all grade levels, and in most curriculum areas.

These categories all overlap somewhat, and in a normal elementary classroom, all four methods might be modified and employed at one time or another to fit needs or objectives.

When first starting out to individualize instruction, the teacher should choose *one* area, and in our case this is remedial reading. At elementary school levels, the individualized approach in remediation should follow the prescriptive techniques described under school-determined pacing and self-directed instruction.

According to Piaget there are developmental stages of the human cognitive processes and these develop within a pattern. A child progresses as he moves along a continuum, one growth stage in developmental reasoning leading to the next stage. These stages do not occur at a certain set *chronological* age, but develop within each child's own growth pattern.

Maturation occurs as part of normal development, while learning occurs *only* after appropriate experiences. Thus, presenting concepts out of sequence can seriously hamper a child's cognitive development (reasoning powers). In fact, in some cases it can cause severe emotional crippling. It is best to broaden or maximize experience at different levels of development so that the child is self-confident and reaches the mastery level for that stage.

As an example, during my elementary school years, my family moved about a great deal. I remember at one school we were just beginning to learn our multiplication tables. We moved—and my class at the new school was working two and three place multiplication and division examples. Here is a classic example of too difficult concepts presented before the student had reached the proper experience level. I was afloat in a sea of numbers, with no life preserver. My mother patiently tutored me on the multiplication tables at home, and both my parents helped me with my homework. Presenting too many or too difficult concepts too soon can negate all instruction and encourage "silent rebellion." It took *years* to overcome the mental block that developed from the experience. (Picture this same type of experience happening to a child in beginning reading!)

Learning Centers and How to Set Them Up

A learning center is an area set aside where materials for one activity or curriculum are displayed and stored for the students' use. It may also provide work space. The function of the learning center is to improve, extend, and enrich the student activities through independent study.

Learning centers should place the responsibility of learning on the *student,* the role of the teacher being one of guidance and direction. The student accepts the burden of responsibility for his actions in following through on the activity or contract. The teacher acts as resource personnel, helping students to learn to focus on one stage of learning. He provides all available materials suitable to the activity or curriculum goal, and helps maintain interest by providing information about other sources and resources for the student. In some cases, he provides answers, or gives lessons pertinent to the curriculum area. (Even when giving a lesson, he is still fulfilling his role as resource personnel or director, but is also putting the learning task where it belongs—with the student.)

There are a variety of ways in which to set up learning centers within a classroom. Each teacher should utilize her space and materials to her utmost advantage. Factors that will affect learning center arrangements are floor plan, cupboard and storage space available, lighting and windows, number of students (amount of room needed for desks, students' personal storage space, etc.), general age and ability range of students, and amount of equipment and supplies available for use.

For instance, a primary reading center might contain dittoed story lessons, arranged sequentially in a file box; listening stations, with earphone headsets and tape recorder for listening to taped stories and lessons; cans or boxes of crayons for story illustration; extra paper and pencils; all of this placed on a work table with adequate seating and work space for a group of four or five.

For students with poor visual association or visual memory skills, or those weak in figure-ground perception, this center could contain simple, taped phonics lessons, complete with work papers to be filled in while listening to tape recorded directions. With this type disability, it would then be necessary to include "fun" exercises, work papers such as embedded figures, complete the picture, or dot-to-dots to match the recorded lesson. (Other perceptual materials you could use are listed in Chapter 5.)

Learning centers need to be bright, interesting, and challenging. Therefore, the amount of equipment and supplies is extremely important to your program. The materials themselves should be challenging enough to make the students want to follow through on learning center activities, yet they should be geared and worded so that the students are able to work independently or with a minimum of guidance. Our goal is *independence.*

When first organizing learning centers and gathering materials, work only on one curriculum area. Start with one learning center or station which may be only a table with reference materials, games, quiet time worksheets, etc., or any activity which motivates the child to learn. The materials should be displayed to fullest advantage, and children encouraged to use them in their allotted time or during free time.

The learning center can also include "contracts" in a separate box. Students who are capable of handling contracts should be encouraged to try advanced materials from the learning center. Those having difficulty can proceed at a slower pace, or learn how to work on simpler contracts.

A contract, as the term implies, is simply an agreement between the teacher and the student. The contract sets forth how much work of a specified nature is to be accomplished within a given length of time. The amount of work, its type, and the materials to be used are agreed upon by the teacher and student. Certain objectives are to be obtained, with the teacher's help and guidance. With remedial students, some reward may be given, such as playing a game with the teacher, when the objectives of the contract are met. In the upper grades, most students are motivated by their internal feelings of success at having fulfilled the contract, and for these, a word of praise from the teacher is usually all that is necessary.

When setting up learning centers for reading, the reading and research materials should incorporate all different levels of reading ability you have noted in the classroom, so that all students, and especially the remedial ones, are motivated to use them. The materials should be simple enough to master, but provide an increment of challenge, so that students learn a little more from each experience, sort of a "carrot in front of the nose" technique.

If space is a problem, try setting up a bulletin board as a learning center, with "pockets" (large envelopes) containing different activities incorporated in the design on the board. Materials can be placed in a nearby cupboard, or the student might be told where to locate his materials via his worksheet or contract. One of my colleagues uses just such an arrangement and has dubbed the learning center the "Workshop Wall."

Since our goal is to improve reading skills, our basic assumption must be that there are students in the class who have little or no reading ability. Individualizing for these students is a "must," because they will profit from the one-to-one relationship. Contracts or independent study programs must be built around each student's weak areas, and beginning activities at the learning centers must be carefully explained. Keep frustration level firmly in mind and make sure that the disabled reader has independent study materials he can master. Success must be the key to each program.

Keep activities within range. Each activity should reinforce skills a student has learned, and provide the opportunity for growth (remediation in a weak area).

Students with reading disabilities are inclined to try independent learning activities from the learning centers that are much too difficult for them. This "cover up" is an attempt to show other students *and themselves* that they can read. Set up individual programs that will provide challenges yet spare the student embarrassment. Blank contracts are one answer.

Each child is given a contract form, then, as a class with the teacher's guidance, needs are discussed. The types of materials available are displayed and talked about. Then "individual conferences" are arranged, so that each student helps determine his own objectives according to his own needs. (See page 139.)

One way to set up individual conferences is to reserve one section of the chalkboard as a "conference" board, where students can sign their names as they finish an assignment or contract, indicating to the teacher those who are ready for further help and attention.

Another method is to use a clipboard, with a sign-up sheet and pencil attached. In this way, each child takes their turn.

Watch for time-wasting here, especially in lower grades. Children must be encouraged to use their time usefully while awaiting their conference. Encourage them to read their library books, complete an assignment in another subject, or work on another activity. Remember, independent study must be *taught.*

The director should keep a small file box at the conference area so that he has notes of each student's progress. A short notation on a file card will help him remember pertinent facts concerning the student's needs, and enable him to provide more materials for the child's project.

A note pad is also convenient. Many times an idea which the teacher might want to utilize later will evolve from a conversation, and if written down at that moment, is available for further reference or investigation. If the note is not put on paper, it might be lost. Remember, you have 31 active bodies demanding your attention in this kind of situation.

As you plan your learning centers, keep in mind "listening centers," and the use of audio-visual equipment. Students are always intrigued by tapes and records, and need to learn to listen to sounds. Audio equipment helps them to learn to listen carefully. (Students can also listen to teacher-made tapes several times, when needed.) The teacher can employ tapes to give entire lessons, to reinforce a weak area for a child, or to give a test. I use the listening center to record phonics lessons for students weak in this area, and have them *listen* for sounds. After the lesson, they can draw pictures of the sounds they heard (example: for *ship*, the *sh* digraph, they might draw a picture of a ship). Another time, the students might use the tape recorder themselves, recording the sounds (words) they had earlier heard on tapes at the listening center.

There are many uses for tapes and record players, and it is up to the individual teacher to decide how best to incorporate these into her individualized program.

Figure 8-1

This is a sample contract designed for use with a second grade, level one reader. The teacher could alter the contract to fit the student's level of ability by leaving rockets 2 and 3 blank, and writing in directions and exercises as needed.

Name: _____

Ride the Rocket (for the week of _____**).**

1. to story "Rocket Ride" (Listening Center)

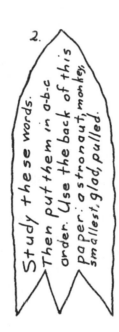

2. Study these words. Then put them in a-b-c order. Use the back of this paper: astronaut, monkey, smallest, glad, pulled.

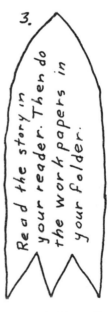

3. Read the story in your reader. Then do the work papers in your folder.

I have completed my contract _____**.**

Teacher's signature _____**.**

Don't overlook the use of *parents* for your learning center activities. Some states have recently enacted laws which encourage and even *mandate* the use of parents in the classroom. For example, California's Early Childhood Education Act (SB 1302) mandates the use of parents, both in planning and implementing instruction.

I have found parents are delighted to be invited into the classroom to help. Even the most hesitant volunteer, when given teacher instruction, can provide essential, valuable services as supervisors and instructors. While working under the teacher's supervision, they also free the teacher to give individual help to other students. These parent aides can tape record lessons, tutor students, type, make dittoes, etc. In fact, in some cases, they have taken over an entire learning unit: setting up the listening activities, giving and checking assignments, planning follow-up lessons, and learning games.

Students can also be taught to use the slide, film strip, and movie projectors, so that they can view materials independently, or in small groups, as part of their learning center activities. Many of the "single concept" films (8 mm.) are available to stimulate creative writing activities, which are basic to a remedial program. You must stimulate the child's imagination, so that he can begin to put what he is learning to use.

Other audio-visual materials which help individualization are charts, maps, filmstrips with accompanying records, pictures mounted on tagboard, story cards, etc. In fact, probably any materials the teacher makes or devises could fit into this category. Teachers need to use their imaginations, too, and devise materials. When you work on these on your own, you are broadening your *own* experience level, avoiding "hum-drum" teaching.

Effective Control with "31" Classes

With each student in a classroom working independently many times the result can be utter chaos. To prevent such an occurrence in your classroom and still maintain an individualized program presents a challenge.

The most effective way to maintain control is to *retain* control from the very beginning. Set your standards for student behavior at the beginning of the program, before students start to use it. Explain the methods, learning centers and their use. Tell what you expect from each student, both in the way of behavior and academic attainment. Cooperation, courtesy, and inter-personal relationships are important to the functioning of the program. The students will cooperate if they know what is expected.

As an example, in my own classroom tasks are assigned on a job card, with lessons keyed to the individual's educational level. The lessons are structured so that most of the material needed are available at his own desk. With a minimum of instruction from the teacher, the students are able to take their job cards from their own assigned pockets on a wall chart. The cards are taken back to their desks, and there the children pursue the tasks allotted to them. Where the materials are not available at their desks, I expect the students to go to the correct cabinet, bookshelf, etc. to obtain their supplies. (All supply cupboards are clearly labeled. Students are not allowed to converge on one certain cupboard or at the library shelf. Instead, signs are posted designating how many students at a time are allowed in the area. This avoids congestion, and keeps traffic paths clear.)

When starting your program, develop a time schedule, with a certain time set aside each day for students to work independently. With a large class, it is best to set up several time slots, when students from different sections of the classroom are free to go to the center for assignments or materials. This is another way to avoid congestion and time-wasting.

While one group of students is gathering materials from the center, another group can be working with an assignment, a third group can be working with the teacher on a lesson, and so on. Organization and planning provide the key to a successful program.

Room organization is extremely important. The learning center should be located within reasonable distance of all students, yet shouldn't obtrude where it becomes inconvenient to large group activities. I find that grouping the student desks in clusters of four or five, with lots of aisle space and a large open area in the center, is the best arrangement for me. The center open space is carpeted, so that children can sit on the floor. The listening center, complete with tape recorder and headphones, is placed along the inner wall. Science and social studies supplies are in a rolling cupboard placed close to the sink, for easy access to water, paints, etc. Study carrels are located across the room, so that noise from the listening center, or from science activities does not bother students wishing to work quietly by themselves.

To a great extent, the permanent fixtures in your classroom will govern the arrangement of the learning centers. Materials and supplies for the learning centers should be organized for easy storage, yet arranged so that students can obtain them with a minimum of assistance from the teacher. I like to keep art supplies, glue, water paints, and paint pans underneath the sink, or in a nearby rolling cupboard. All math supplies, with flashcards, rulers, work papers, and math games, are kept in and on another cupboard. Reading and language arts are located close to the listening center, as these subject matter areas lend themselves easily to listening center activities.

At this point a comment should be made on "housekeeping." Students should be taught that equipment and supplies are stored neatly, and all equipment should be put away in its proper place when they are finished or when the time is up for the day. This should be stressed when setting your behavioral objectives with the class.

With an individual program, record keeping is a must. Records should be kept on each child's progress. Pre- and post-tests are valuable, and each child should know his progress. Involve the students in setting their goals, and let them know their attainments as they move along in the program. In my classroom, using the conference board and file card technique

A WORLD OF IDEAS FOR YOU

Figure 8-2

Sample contract. This "world" is adaptable, and can be used for long-term projects in social studies, science, etc. I designed it to use for individualized instruction.

has been most successful. Students sign up for their conferences and are invited to my "conference station" as their turn comes up on the board. I do not use my desk, preferring a closer one-to-one contact. The desk provides an emotional barrier between the teacher and student, and I find I can have closer rapport with just a chair arrangement or with the student standing beside me while we talk.

Needless to say, many more activities and exercises are needed in an independent study program to provide for all levels, and provide activities while students are working at the learning stations, or with the teacher. You must organize and prepare for *all* students in the classroom, so that each has a project to work on during the time allotted. This helps maintain discipline, reduces noise, and eliminates boredom, the prime cause of misbehavior.

How to Meet Your Goals and Keep Your Sanity

Teaching should be a challenging, stimulating emotional experience, both for the teacher and her students. (Nobody said it would be easy!) The key to a successful, individualized program is the teacher. Her enthusiasm, desire to help students learn, and her attitude toward the students and their work is infectious. Students will sense her degree of rapport, and in turn are challenged and stimulated. The work is exhausting—you will have 31 challenges. It is up to you to make the most of it.

The first step in keeping your sanity and avoiding hum-drum teaching is to change your teaching style. If you do not find a challenge and cannot change yourself, how can you challenge your students?

The factor of greatest worth to you is organization. This means organization of learning materials, your classroom layout, record keeping, and long term planning. The latter is by far the most important.

Ask yourself these questions: What do you want your students to learn? How many areas can you individualize? What

CONTRACT CHECK SHEET

STUDENT: _____

WEEK OF: _____

SUBJECT	CONTRACT NO.	CLASSWORK	BEHAVIOR	EFFORT	COMMENTS	TEACHER INITIAL
		GOOD FAIR POOR	GOOD FAIR POOR	GOOD FAIR POOR		
		GOOD FAIR POOR	GOOD FAIR POOR	GOOD FAIR POOR		
		GOOD FAIR POOR	GOOD FAIR POOR	GOOD FAIR POOR		
		GOOD FAIR POOR	GOOD FAIR POOR	GOOD FAIR POOR		
		GOOD FAIR POOR	GOOD FAIR POOR	GOOD FAIR POOR		
		GOOD FAIR POOR	GOOD FAIR POOR	GOOD FAIR POOR		

Parent Comments: _____

Figure 8-3

Sample contract check sheet for record keeping. This sheet could easily be revised to fit the needs of both upper and lower elementary grades, and can be used in any subject content area. Check sheet is devised to fit standard 8½ by 11 inch ditto paper.

materials do you have available? How much time each week do you wish to devote to the learning center or individualized program. What is the attitude of your administrator or principal? Last, but most important, how much time are *you* willing to put into the program?

Once these questions are answered, you can begin to work out strategies for teaching and learning using learning centers, contracts, and an individualized approach. The key to a successful program for your students is to keep them busy, happy, and moving ahead, each at his own pace. Each child may move in a different direction or be moving at a different level. You may have students using 31 different types of reading materials. Some students—especially reluctant readers—will need to be prodded from time to time, but even these will make progress. Provide materials they can read, and at their *interest* level, and you have overcome half the problem.

Prepare for a noisier classroom. When children are busy and happy, they tend to relax and talk more. However, if your classroom behavior standards have been set at the beginning of the program, then you will be able to control the noise level, and regain the students' attention for entire group activities on signal.

When a child comes to you, on his own, completed project in hand and says, "Teacher, can I have a new contract?"—this makes it all worthwhile.

9

Coordinating Your Remedial Reading Program with Other Subject Areas

We might call this chapter "Putting it all together," because that's what it's all about. I believe there should, indeed there *must,* be continuity within the daily program. Lessons in each content area should correlate within a framework for the entire day's activities. It makes more sense to have carry-over and reinforcement for all curriculum areas, rather than compartmentalize for each subject. Also, in elementary school, it is easier for the child to learn if there seems to be some relationship between all the activities for the day. This is not to say variety is not needed, but to stress the need for a cohesive basic program.

Reading in the Content Areas

A basic premise is that reading should be

taught as a part of communication. A child cannot learn to read without having learned basic listening and speaking skills beforehand, therefore the practicing teacher must utilize these skills in teaching the child to read. Language patterns are developed at preschool age and the teacher must capitalize on them. By utilizing listening, speaking, reading, and writing skills, the teacher helps the child develop an over-all method of communication. Language arts skills are employed in all these areas, and it necessarily follows that better communication skills will be developed by use of an integrated lesson plan idea. Developed further, the concept readily expands to include teaching communication skills in the content areas, such as math, social studies, health, and so on.

Most students do not realize that to read successfully in content areas, a different kind of skill (approach) is needed. That is, we read fast when reading a story book for fun, but must slow down when reading a set of directions or learning a new concept. Ergo, *speed* of reading is dependent on the type of material involved. You will notice that when reading a recipe you sometimes re-read a part several times in order to follow the directions and insure success in the final product. This is also the case in reading in the content areas.

Presently, most textbooks in other curriculum areas are written using vocabulary one grade level below the basic reading level for that grade. For example, except for some specialized vocabulary, social studies texts in third grade use vocabulary taught at second grade level. This is for easier mastery of content and generalizations, so that students do not have to contend with "frustration level" vocabulary. Most new terms are introduced in context within the framework of the chapter. In some of the newer publications, there is also provision for individual differences. By use of limited vocabulary and different types of lessons, assignments can be given and lessons or units can be compiled that meet the needs of a particular classroom. Teachers can choose one unit without moving in sequence through the entire text. Most social studies and science volumes contain more material than any one teacher can "cover" adequately in one year. There is an over-supply to allow for teaching what might be pertinent, and to provide content that lends itself to a teacher's special interests. Thus he can capitalize on his own experience, interests, and specialties and can teach to students' basic interests and needs.

I have seen a whole class become interested in some subject and take off "like a rocket" in a unit of study. A few years back, long before the present ecology boom, I started out to teach a unit on conservation, a special interest area of my own. We had had an exceedingly hard winter for northern California. While studying migration in connection with weather changes, we became involved in feeding the starving birds in our area which did *not* migrate. Our ecology unit soon turned into a study unit on birds. Before we were through, the whole class had made bird feeders, written stories about birds, drawn bird pictures, made ceramic wind chimes to decorate the porch or patio and had gone on field trips to watch birds in wild life sanctuaries. Many students built back yard mini-refuges and became interested in bird watching. Several read books they would not have been able to read three months before, indeed, they wouldn't even have looked for them in the library.

How many different content areas were involved? Social studies (ecology, kindness to animals, etc.); science (nature study, migration patterns, feathers and flight, seasons, geography); arts and crafts (bird feeders made from milk cartons, wind chimes made from clay and "found" materials); language arts via story writing and letters to the Nature Conservancy (a project in itself); library research and reference skills (learning to use the card catalog to find books); reading (use of new vocabulary; and spelling (by using new terms, phrases, etc.). Perception exercises were stressed by use of hidden pictures and "dot-to-dot" puzzles of birds to help students with perceptual handicaps. Thus all curriculum areas were tied together.

Were the children learning? You can bet they were—and they loved it! Can it be done at all grade levels? Yes, I've carried it through successfully at all of them, and you can, too.

Traditional vs. "Open" Classroom

What is an "open" classroom? How does it differ from a traditional classroom? What techniques are employed there and what materials are used? How do we evaluate learning? Does it lend itself to the idea of coordinating curriculum?

The basic difference in methodology between a traditional, or regular, classroom and the open classroom is the shift in emphasis from *teaching* to *learning*. As stated elsewhere, the goal is to teach the child to "learn how to learn." The way we reach this goal then becomes the most important part of the learning process.

The concept of informal education (or "open" planning) developed in England over 30 years ago. The focus became child-centered rather than academically-oriented, and was based on the belief that children should be excited about what they learn and should be happy during the process.

The key to open planning is diversity. The child should be comfortable in his school environment. There is no set permanent seating arrangement, and groups change as their learning activities change. Learning stations are utilized and there is an extensive use of "found" materials.

Open classrooms are usually noisier than a traditional classroom. When children are happy and relaxed, they tend to become talkative. This is annoying to some teachers, and those familiar with traditional methods find the noise and extra activity difficult to tolerate at first and discover that students are a little more difficult to control. The traditional plan would

Figure 9-1

This is a layout of an open classroom for students ten to 11 years old. (Dimensions of classroom: approximately 25 by 30 feet.) Plenty of open space has been left to accommodate freedom of movement. Rugs, pillows, and comfortable chairs are recommended for the quiet corner.

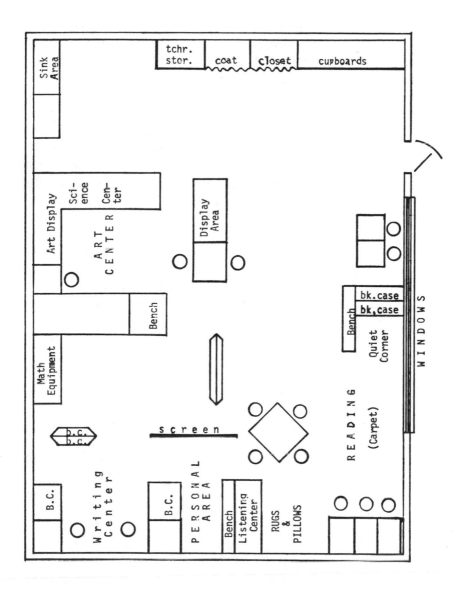

probably be better for teachers finding the open classroom a difficult situation.

Most open classroom resemble workshops perhaps more than a regular classroom, with "learning stations" set up at different locations. The teacher acts as a director or guide (resource person) to facilitate learning and give the child more freedom to discover answers on his own.

This is not to say that students working in open classrooms are utterly free to do anything they want. They must have controlled freedom, the allowance to operate in a "structured" framework. Guidelines must be set and basic objectives for the students kept in mind. With too much freedom, the child becomes worried and anxious, as he doesn't know exactly what is expected of him. With too little, the child becomes thwarted and frustrated in his attempts to learn. The centers and the directors themselves cannot be aimless, but must have a learning objective on which the child can focus. In addition, students need to help set goals for themselves, for their learning projects, and thus learn to follow through and complete the tasks.

Open planning requires a different attitude on the part of the teacher. She must become more accepting, less judging. As facilitator or "director," she must be constantly moving in and out of groups; guiding, directing, suggesting, motivating, answering questions, and directing toward the next step or next activity.

How the teacher makes knowledge available is the key to discipline (boredom factor). A child who becomes deeply involved in a project is less apt to get into mischief because the project demands his attention.

In an open classroom, the group must be able to come together at times as an entire class for some activities: discussion, evaluation, whole class projects, etc. This allows the teacher to get feedback, an important evaluation tool in this organizational plan. The open classroom allows flexibility in grouping, as the less able child can work with younger students, while a more able child can work with older ones (within his own maturity level) for challenge and satisfaction of his needs.

In non-graded open classroom in England and the United States, younger children seem to settle down to quiet activities faster as they see examples of older children working. I also found this to be true in teaching combination classes, and "cross grade" teaching seems to support the theory.

Providing for Individual Differences

This book focuses on remediation in reading, so the intent is to involve the slower students into all the activities possible. Thus, when planning lessons, be sure to include plans, ideas, and materials for different levels, so that slower students can learn and succeed at the same time your more able students are challenged.

Most textbooks in other curriculum areas provide only minimal suggestions for meeting individual needs, so it is up to the teacher to take suggestions offered, amplify them, and then add her own so that coordinating curriculum within the plan's framework is feasible. This may entail setting up blank contracts, or varying activities via verbal directions. Vocabulary should be kept simple, with new terms added at the correct learning rate for each child. New concepts and generalizations must be *paced*, to fit the learning capabilities of each child, adding and reinforcing at a slower rate for the remedial students.

An important fact to remember is that children learn from other children. There is a great interchange of ideas as students share information. Often, the slower child will approach a problem from a new angle and apply different methods to find solutions. Since he doesn't read well, he has learned to look and listen in an effort to learn more.

While this is a well-known fact, it is sometimes overlooked or forgotten in the press for learning. These students often have a great deal to contribute. Many of your reluctant readers have oral language deficits, so they especially need to be allowed time to talk and present their ideas. Involve these students who aren't comfortable in reading by bringing your entire class together for a discussion of projects. Having students evaluate their own work is an excellent way to help *all* students develop self-confidence, and the feeling of being an important part of the group.

How to Plan a Curriculum Coordinated Schedule

For effective correlation of reading and language skills, start with the teachers' manuals for these subject matter areas when you are ready to begin your day's or week's lesson plan. Each lesson or day's work is but a part of your program, so the first step of the day is planning your review of the previous day's lessons (follow-up). Be sure to include this at the beginning of your daily plan, then lead into your activities with new material. The key is to start with a basal reader text for one group and choose from it the lesson or concept (learning skill). Then find the same concept in your other readers for the other groups.

For children not using a regular text but who are working with you individually, make up a lesson they can master which will tie in with the rest of the class' plan for the day. This way the concept is not new when they see it in another curriculum area. Transfer and reinforcement of learning is extremely important for these students. The more they practice with a new concept or learning skill, the better they will grasp it.

After planning for reading skills, check related language activities. It is easier to find lessons in English, spelling, and social studies than in other curriculum areas, so start at the easiest point. I suggest language arts. Select a lesson that will complement or reinforce the concept you've planned for reading and check for new or different vocabulary which must be presented. After setting up the plan for this area, be sure the seat work follows through to again reinforce the concept. I think a word about seat work is in order. Students' written work should serve a definite purpose, and that purpose is *not* to keep them in their seats! Unless these assignments tie in to your program they are a waste of time, both for the students and for you.

Move to your next curriculum area, and again, with your primary objective reading, look for materials to reinforce the reading concept. Terminology and vocabulary may be very different in these areas, so special care must be taken to insure that all students, especially the reluctant readers, can recognize and *understand* the meanings of the new words and phrases. In upper elementary grades, both nouns and verbs and subjects and predicates could be integrated into your correlated language arts and reading lesson. During social studies, have students look for the main idea in each paragraph, as they do in reading. You'll be pleasantly surprised at how much this improves their *understanding* of the social studies content. (Remember that the chart in Chapter 3 shows that most reading skills are taught in lower grades, while upper elementary concentrates on sharpening word attack skills and learning to read for meaning and content.)

As you move on to spelling, introduce lessons that pertain and again, reinforce the basic topic for the lesson plan's sequence. Pick a lesson stressing the same types of learnings, and as seat work activities, devise tasks that will aid the reinforcement process. For abler students, include "bonus" words from social studies or language arts. For those less able, who might be using different texts or different spelling lists, plan reinforcement activities to fit their needs and to carry out the main idea of the target concept. They still need to be part of the group at the same time they are working to improve their specific disabilities.

All students, and especially reluctant readers, need to enrich and broaden their vocabulary. I have found a vocabulary builder that meets the needs of the classroom and at the same time motivates the students in creative writing. Starting in September and for each month thereafter, I have a monthly word list on the chalkboard. I elicit these words from the students, and build the list around events and activities that pertain to the current month. All words come from the students, and are therefore already in their speaking vocabulary. By using these words in their creative writing assignments, they become part of their reading and writing vocabulary. These words are added to during the month, at the students' request and as the need arises. If *you* try it, you'll find that most of your time during the creative writing period will be spent at the chalkboard, spelling words correctly for the students to use. The students' enthusiasm for this method is contagious, and they vie with each other to give pertinent words to be listed on the chalkboard. It also gives an insight into the students' interests and at the same time gives you a pretty good idea of their attainment level. Try decorating the "September Words" area with colored chalk. Draw simple cartoons applicable to the fall season. Colored leaves are fun and easy to draw. Watch the students' eyes light up, and in the ensuing months, watch them try to "second guess" you, as to what color of chalk and what theme you will use. It's easy to turn the "O" in October into a jack-o-lantern. It's a fun learning situation and the students can really get involved!

Handwriting skills will fall naturally into place in this scheme, so little needs to be said here. Just include words from the day's lessons or from the monthly word list as students work on letter formation. However, be *sure* to observe students with perceptual disabilities so they get help if needed for correct letter formation, angle of paper, posture and so on. In fact, posture is most important for *all* students as it aids letter formation and ease of writing. Incidentally, many students get calluses on their middle finger. This is an indication that they are holding their pencils too tightly. The teacher should be able to stand behind the student and easily pull the pencil from his grasp. This indicates the student is holding the writing instrument correctly and is relaxed enough to do a good job in letter formation.

"The left-handed child in a right-handed world usually has difficulty developing an acceptable sensory-motor posture (for handwriting)," says Dr. Robert M. Wold.[1] During normal writing the left-hander must *pull* the pencil across the paper, rather than push it as a right-hander does, thus the child must develop a completely opposite motor development in the arm. To prevent adverse adaptation, specific individualized instruction must be given to these children. As a natural consequence of correct motor development, the left-handed student when writing correctly should develop a vertical or "backhand" slope

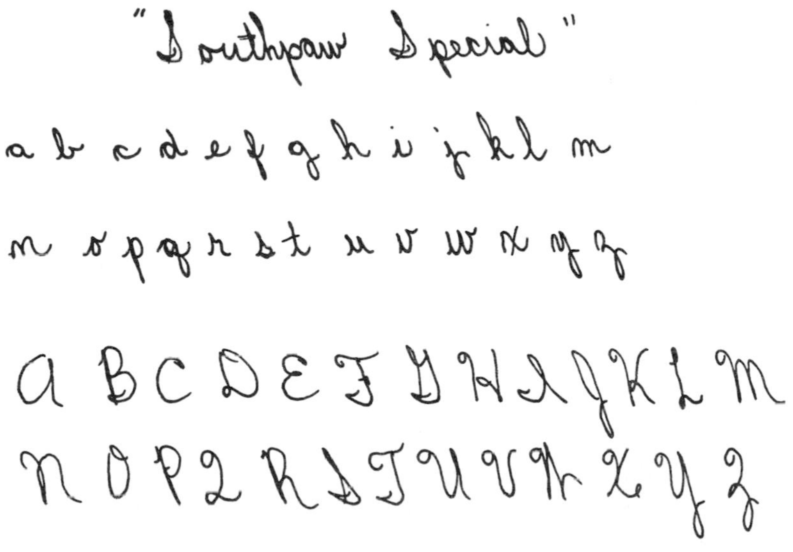

Figure 9-2

Handwriting model for left-handed students. According to Dr. Wold, the student's paper should slant in a line parallel to the elbow and forearm, with the bottom right-hand corner centered directly in front of the student.

[1] Robert M. Wold, O.D., *SCREENING TESTS to be Used by the Classroom Teacher* (1539 Fourth Street, San Rafael, California 94901: Academic Therapy Publications, 1970), p. 33.

to his writing.[2] This idea may sound far-fetched to those among you who teach handwriting, but I have tried it in my own classroom with second grade left-handed students. By placing their paper at the proper slant, with the paper running parallel to their left elbows, the students' writing developed into a natural backhand.

While it may be more difficult to correlate math or science activities into your over-all program, attempts should be made to do this wherever possible. Today's trend toward flexibility in learning situations for students may facilitate matters some. However, the burden still falls on you as classroom teacher to pull all the areas together to fit your classroom needs. Students with reading disability may be more able in numerical concepts, and thus have more success here. Don't forget there are also the old familiar "story problems" to worry about. Disabilities in reading or conceptualization skills will rise to the surface here. I find most students at any grade level, regardless of reading ability, have difficulty with word problems. Be sure they know what the problem *asks*. What information are they trying to find from the facts given? All students will profit from lessons in how to read word problems in math.

The same is also true of science curriculum. Students need to be shown what data are relevant to certain problems or experiments. This again is a basic reading skill that must be taught. Your students don't just absorb this. Work to help them understand how to read for information that will aid them.

A coordinated curriculum program has many advantages. Chief among these are continuity, reinforcement, and relevance to the target area. The program should be consistent and cohesive. That is, each lesson in any curriculum area should have the same general focus, integrating it into the entire day's plan. By "zeroing in" on a major focus, all lessons have a cumulative effect.

Another advantage to the program is the evaluation which can be done. By using a coordinated program you can get a

---

[2]*Ibid*, p. 34.

good cross-section of the child's work, and can evaluate progress across a wide spectrum. You can tell where the concept is getting across.

This is also a good check on how *well* you as a teacher are expressing the concept. Sometimes teacher evaluation is more important than student evaluation. If you see that many children are having difficulty with the concept, then it probably needs to be retaught, either as a small group lesson or with the whole class.

Keep the basic premise in mind—continuity of the day's or week's program. Have a definite objective. *What* do you want your students to learn? In what major curriculum areas can you teach or reinforce the concept? What extra materials or teaching aids might be helpful? What materials will the students need? How should the concept be presented initially? When these questions are answered, you are well on your way to a curriculum coordinated lesson plan.

Sample Lesson Plan

A typical day's program for a reluctant reading group could be planned this way: in the following correlated lessons only one new concept is introduced, the spelling of the sound of "k" . . . that is, use *k* in spelling one syllable words before "e" or "i" and *c* before most of the other letters. Example: kill, keen, kick, keep, but care, core, clean, crush, etc. The initial concept is presented in the reading lesson, and then reinforced in the related spelling lesson, and on into English. In this way, the basic concept is presented in several different areas, utilizing the textbooks to stimulate both transfer of learning and mastery of the concept. *Learning objective for the day:* To introduce to sound and spelling of "k"; to reinforce and review sounds of "b", "d", "t", "p" and "g". (The students are to be aware that there are two separate spellings for the sound of "k" at the beginning of a word.)

Reading Lesson. Use a prepared phonics review of words

beginning with these separate sounds at the beginning of words. Then, elicit from the group words which end in sounds of "b," "d," etc. If the students have the ability, then work with these letters in medial position. While most students can give words in initial and final position, they find it very difficult to pluck out of thin air words which have the consonants in medial position. So it is usually better to give many concrete examples of words with the target consonants in medial position and have students *locate* these. Incorporate motor action wherever possible. Have students come to the chalkboard and point out or underline the consonant letters. Active participation aids learning, and increases motivation. After the lesson, individual practice in workbooks or a dittoed work paper should be used as a follow-up activity. When the paper or workbook is gone over the following day, the student is provided additional practice by checking his work. The key to learning with reluctant readers is constant reinforcement and maintenance of skills learned, so that one concept is not forgotten when a new one is introduced. For example, in the reading story for the day, students should encounter and identify the words containing the target consonants. The teacher points out the words, and then elicits more from the students.

English Lesson. Sounds and spelling of English words. The rules for figuring out sounds and spelling are given in many of our "linguistic" type texts. The Roberts English series, for example, gives the rules for use of "c" and "k" in initial position.

Spelling Lesson. List for the week should include many one syllable words with the sound of "k." Both "c" and "k" words in should be included, so that students get more practice in the target area. (For the spelling lesson, use "c" and "k" words in *initial* position only. The "k" sound at the end of the word is usually spelled "ck." and will cause confusion if stressed at this time.)

Handwriting Lesson. Use this lesson to point out the configuration of the letters "c" and "k." Emphasize correct letter formation; height, spacing, etc. Point out similarities in the letters "l."

"b," and "k." The students thus are reviewing and maintaining the previous sounds and are getting added practice in the new target sound ("k"). Cull words for the handwriting lesson from the lessons in reading, spelling, and English.

This lesson was originally planned for fifth grade. I correlated it with the unit on the original 13 colonies, and utilized use of words like *C*ontinental *C*ongress, *c*onstitution, and *c*olonies. The use of "k" spelling was presented in the story of Benjamin Franklin, with the use of *k*ite and *k*ey.

The art lesson for the week was the making of Indian masks relating to the tribes which were near the colonies and were friends with the colonists. (If this unit were to be presented in the spring, you could substitute kite-making as an arts and crafts lesson.)

10

Tested Games and Activities That Increase Individual Reading Skills

Teachers are the best "scavengers" around. They diligently look for new materials for games for their classrooms.

Students with reading disabilities have short attention spans and are easily frustrated, so many varied activities are needed to help strengthen basic skills. Games provide motivation and are a fun way to learn. In games the student doesn't feel frustrated, but is relaxed and comfortable at his learning tasks. To him, it *is* a game; to the teacher, more positive reinforcement in certain skills areas.

Games, like the open classroom and the individualized instructional approach, cannot just be "there." Definite purposes for different types of games must be the focus. Activities must be incorporated which enhance the learning procedure, at the same time insuring success.

163

Do not use your game drawer only for "rainy day" activities. Periodically have a reading "games day" or one for math. (Remember, math problems are another area requiring reading and use of different vocabulary.) Plan the day as a complete surprise to the students, so that they do not know in advance. It's more fun that way.

In my own program reading games include all kinds of phonics, vocabulary, and word games, while math includes card games, flashcards, dominoes, checkers, tangrams, and different kinds of gameboards from commercial toy stores. Dominoes and checkers stimulate critical creative thinking and visual sequential memory skills, and improve manual dexterity and motor control. The original tangram puzzle, consisting of seven pieces, originated in China, and is currently enjoying a new wave of popularity. I use it to reinforce mathematical concepts and to help students visualize relationships. The activities are open-ended, and are adaptable to children at all grade levels. At our school, tangrams are begun in kindergarten, and are used up through grade six. (See page 165.)

Many materials can be bought cheaply right after seasonal displays, such as Christmas. Take advantage of these "clearance bargains" to stock up your classroom, and check rummage sales, "flea markets" and so on for outgrown games that are being discarded.

Another source for games is your students. Have them bring their own from home to share with the class. Most have one or two that they can "donate" for the school year, and they will enjoy sharing a favorite game with classmates. Parents are usually willing to donate outgrown games and activities to schools and classrooms.

Don't forget puppets or bean bag activities. Students like

Figure 10-1

These are the shapes of the seven Tangram pieces. Reproduced from the *TANGRAMATH,* by Dale Seymour, Creative Publications, Inc., P.O. Box 10328, Palo Alto, California 94303.

THE TANGRAM SHAPES

THESE ARE
THE SEVEN
TANGRAM PIECES!

PLACE YOUR TANGRAM PIECES
ON THE SHAPES ABOVE

(IF YOU DON'T HAVE A SET OF TANGRAM SHAPES,
YOU MAY WANT TO MAKE YOUR OWN FROM THE
PATTERNS ABOVE.)

to make up puppet plays, and the experience of writing out parts, then memorizing and acting them out is a good way to stimulate reading.

My own students "thought up" a bean bag game on their own. They would select a letter, such as *b*. As each child took a turn at tossing, he would have to say a word beginning with *b* sound. If correct, he got his points, and if he missed, he lost a turn. (This is not as painful as it sounds, because bystanders are always helpful in supplying word and letter combinations. Most children in the early grades like to help each other.)

Jigsaw puzzles and manipulative games help students with motor control problems. Jigsaw puzzles also help students with visual perceptual problems. Hand-eye coordination and muscle balance are very important skills to develop for all children, and especially for those with perceptual problems.

During games, allow students to use all of the room. Desks should be ignored as much as possible—the floor is usually better. Remember, "Games Day" should be fun, so give your students freedom to enjoy it.

Types of Games and Activities That
Reinforce Reading Skills

There are commercially-made games to reinforce learning skills available through different basal reader publishers. In the teachers' manuals, there are games the teachers can make to fit individual needs.

Primary level students enjoy games like Lotto, Bingo, Junior Scrabble, etc., and simple games where they can move their "pieces" along a game board. Games that I have devised along this line and that are included here are "Road Race" and "Keep Away." Other games that I have found helpful are Dolch's "Popper Words," "Wordo," and for upper grades, commercial games like "Monopoly," "Parcheesi," and "Yahtzee" are excellent. These have cards with them that must be read to follow instructions. They provide reinforcement of reading skills and a painless way to learn new words.

Many ideas suggested in the teachers' manuals, especially at upper grades, are paper-and-pencil-type activities. Students with problems will often need visual, motor, and tactile activities, and they do not respond well to these types of games. They need to get their whole bodies involved in the learning process. Frustration seems to generate one of two things—excess energy or complete apathy! They either clown around or disturb their neighbors, or just sit and occupy a chair. Either way, involving students so that hands, bodies, and minds are all at work will insure a more successful program.

When working with one student or a small group, include a game as one of the tasks or activities for reinforcement of the concept. Utilize your game drawer to its utmost advantage.

Games for Tactile Motor Development

Hand-eye coordination is improved by training in large and small muscle activities. A wide variety of manipulative activities keep the child interested, free from boredom and restlessness, and helps develop better coordination conducive to better reading skills. "Finger plays," singing games, and physical activities such as jumping rope are effective. Within the classroom use jigsaw puzzles and manipulative games like "Tiddly-Winks," "Jackstraws," "Jacks," and "Chinese Checkers." Plays and simple dramatic productions and charades appeal to all grade levels, and are excellent for both visual sequential memory (by learning parts), and improvement of body control. Here are some advantages of tactile motor activities:

1. Builds a better self-image—something these children *can* do successfully.
2. Siphons off excess energy without frustrating the child.
3. Provides richer, broader experience levels.
4. Use as "warm-up" and "follow-up" activities with reading lessons.

5. Can be utilized in a curriculum coordinated approach, tying together different subject matter areas.

Visual Perceptual Games

Any game that improves hand-eye coordination also improves visual perception. Games such as dominoes where children must match like objects are helpful. The "License Plate" game is especially good for visual sequential memory. Also, "What's Missing?" and "Merry Mix-up" are good activities.

For primary grades, simple card games like "Old Maid" and "Fish," where matching the cards is the objective, are effective and fun for the students. In primary grades, sets of cards where students must match pictures can be made quickly and easily on tagboard. Picture and sound games can also be devised. Put a picture cut out of a magazine on one piece of tagboard. Put a beginning sound on another of the same size. The child must match the two to get a point.

As mentioned earlier, hidden pictures and dot-to-dot activities for seat work are also good motivators, and keep the students interested. Most students like to work mazes. Try having the whole class make their own mazes as an art project. Making mazes with straight lines makes an excellent ruler activity (building manipulative skill). Then have students exchange and work each others' mazes. This is a fun project, and *all* the students, regardless of reading level, can get involved.

Listening Skills

Since the advent of T.V. most youngsters have learned to live within a noisier environment. They automatically "screen out" the background noise and listen for information or pertinent material. However, some children cannot pick out the key sounds embedded within the rest of the noise. These children need more ear training to listen for the key sounds.

This can be done through games, especially singing games and records. Have students listen for repeated sounds or phrases in music from a record. You can also tape record common sounds, such as the school bus pulling out of the parking lot, the sound of a light switch being turned on and off, etc., and use them as guessing games, either with the whole class or at a listening center.

Some of the newer audio-visual "talking toys" which are commercially manufactured employ a Show-and-Tell technique which make them especially beneficial as listening devices. An example is "Show 'N Tell," manufactured by General Electric Corporation.

Outdoor games which are beneficial are "Mother, May I?," "Simon Says," and the use of jump rope songs. Indoors, for rainy days, use "Dog and the Bone," or "Gossip," or use as a whole class activity "Where Am I?." This exercise will improve listening skills for all. "Simon Says" can be used either as an indoor or outdoor activity.

Phonics games, in which students must respond with a designated sound, such as *p* in the beginning, medial, or final position, are very helpful. The bean bag game described earlier in the chapter is very effective. Another one is "Grocery Store," which is included in the games at the end of this chapter.

"Memory tapes" can be recorded. These can be used as an entire class activity or at a listening center. Record on tape a series of numbers—short at first, consisting of only two or three in series. Pause. The child or class must write down the number sequence he hears. The next series of numbers is given, and the child writes again. Be sure to allow ample time for the child to write the numbers before starting the next series. I also use this method to give dictation spelling tests in my classroom. First, I give the entire sentence, so students can hear the material in context. Then I break the sentence into meaningful phrases as I dictate out loud. Students then write the phrases as I dictate. After dictation, I repeat the sentence, so the students can check their writing. Using this method improves listening skills and at the same time is another step in coordinating curriculum, tying together reading (via the listening skill), handwriting, and spelling.

Entire Class Activities

Many of the activities already discussed in this chapter are adaptable to entire classes. The major objective in our case is to provide a fun way to learn.

Again, it is a good idea to coordinate curriculum as much as possible. Utilize physical education exercises and arts and crafts periods to improve hand-eye coordination and body control.

For language expression deficits, class discussions during the social studies period will increase verbal expression and help students learn to focus on the main idea or topic. Most teachers read stories aloud to their students (either periodically or two or three times a week). I use my story time in two ways. First, I review with students what has happened before, eliciting story sequence and motivating for the rest of the story or the day's reading. The other way stimulates outside reading. I will begin a new story or a new book. Then after reading the first few paragraphs, or in a story book the first chapter, I tell the class, "You'll have to finish reading it for yourself." This encourages students to do more independent reading. Always be sure the book you choose is the correct grade level for your students, or perhaps even a little below, and that the story line moves quickly. Also, remember to use lots of expression in *your* oral reading. Make the book exciting so students will want to read it. Students also like to get a book the teacher has read aloud and re-read it for themselves. Make sure a copy or two is available for them after you have finished reading a book to them. It's surprising how many will then re-read the book for themselves. This again gives more practice in reading.

Crossword puzzles are excellent activities. Start with very simple ones, so that your disabled readers can master them easily. You can make up your own using the Dolch list, or use your spelling list for the week. You can also use those published commercially in connection with basal readers and other curriculum materials. Another good source are the activity books and puzzle books you can buy at drug and variety stores. One caution in using puzzles should be mentioned. Most children, especially in primary grades, haven't the faintest notion of what a crossword puzzle is all about! They have to be *shown* that it is a set of meanings for which they must guess the words. They must be *told* how to work the letters across, and to count how many spaces, so they will know how many letters are in the word. This is a *skill* which must be taught. Therefore, be sure to start with very simple crosswords, with only a few words to figure out on a sheet. Work through the first few puzzles with the students, either by putting an entire puzzle on the chalkboard, or by flashing it on a screen with an overhead projector, so that the entire group can learn the skill. It's surprising how many elementary school students do not understand how to work crossword puzzles, and think them intricate and mysterious. I teach them as a skill in second grade, and in past years of teaching have discovered many fifth and sixth grade students didn't know how to work them, especially those with reading problems.

There are several commercial publications I have found helpful, and which will help you make crossword puzzles and other games. One of these is *Individualized Reading Skills Improvement*[1], which is especially made for the classroom teacher to tear out pages to ditto copies of the exercises. These include word circles, set-ups for simple crossword puzzles, and other activities easily adaptable to individuals, small groups or the entire class.

Another good activity to stimulate students is "Complete the Picture" (see examples at end of chapter). Give the students a sheet of paper with a circle, or one or two lines, etc. Tell them the picture is started but not complete. Have them use their

---

[1] Alfred A. Artuso and others, *Individualized Reading Skills Improvement* (Denver, Colorado 80222: Love Publishing Co.).

imaginations and add lines, color, and so on to complete the drawing in their own way. This is a challenging activity and the students thoroughly enjoy it.

As a written exercise you can use "complete the story" techniques. Give students the beginning of a story, and have them finish writing what they think happened. Conversely, once in a while it is fun to give students the ending—then have them fill in the beginning and the middle.

Another technique for story writing is to give three entirely unrelated objects, such as a roller skate, a plum, and a nickel. Then the students are to take these three words and weave them into a story. Another idea is to tie these to your monthly word list, as mentioned in Chapter 9.

Entire class activities should be stimulating creative experiences for all students in the class. Choose games, exercises, and activities that are stimulating and fun. Opportunities here for experimentation on the teacher's part are boundless. Make the most of them.

Individual or Small Group Activities

One of the main concerns with the individual or small group approach is complete rapport. With a smaller, more intimate atmosphere teachers can work to build more self-confidence. I cannot emphasize too strongly the feelings of the student. *He needs to know you care.*

The best way to individualize your program is to find a child's particular interest and work through this channel. If he is interested in baseball, think of all the words you know about the sport, then devise a game using these words. You can make up a crossword puzzle, or look for a dot-to-dot ditto, or use complete the picture techniques described earlier. Another recreational device is to help the child find books in the school library that pertain to his interest and are on his reading level.

"Keep Away Words," "Word Ladders," "Funny Phrases," and "Silly Sentences" are all games I have devised to work with students individually or in small groups. The ideas are not new, and even the titles have probably been used by other teachers somewhere, but the idea remains the same. These are all excellent activities which incorporate both basic sight words and phonics techniques to build vocabulary.

Most of the games and techniques mentioned in this chapter can easily be modified to fit needs of individuals, small groups or the entire class. Indeed, many of the training techniques given in Chapters 5 and 6 are also useful. There are many more materials available commercially; and with more emphasis on the open classroom, more are being published every year. Many times, by just looking at some of these publications, or viewing materials in the catalogs, you will think of games to make up on your own. Devise your own techniques by varying those you see print. Take ideas you get from your reading workbooks and adapt them for individual use.

Almost any material the teacher presents to her class will be accepted if it is presented as a game. Learning activities needn't be dull. The key to *all* these activities is teacher enthusiasm. On Games Day, *play with them*, don't just sit there! Get involved! If the students feel that you think it's fun, then the mood is infectious. Make the games a challenge—but also make them stimulating, exciting, and fun.

Selected Games

Most games have to be *taught*. We expect students to come to school knowing how to play checkers, dominoes, and the like, and take it for granted that most children have these games at home. In many cases, this is far from the truth, especially for students from educationally-deprived homes. Sometimes the games they use at school are the only ones they see. Since they *don't* have games at home, it is well to go over the rules, or play the game with them once or twice so they can learn how the game is played.

The games suggested in this section were not selected at

random, but were chosen to enhance curriculum and motivate students, while improving or strengthening certain skills. The list is not complete, but should act as a springboard so that teachers can collect and devise their own games to meet classroom needs. The games are listed in the order mentioned in the chapter, along with skills areas they specifically help strengthen. Those not listed were previously described in earlier chapters.

Road Race

Supplies needed: Large sheet of colored tagboard (18" x 24"), eight small cars to use as markers, one pair of dice.

Make a game board by dividing off 2" square sections. Decorate the edges, center, etc. with pictures of cars, trucks, and motorcycles, checkered flags, pit stops, and so on. In the squares print consonant letters digraphs and blends. (Cover the board with clear Con-Tact paper or laminate with plastic so the board doesn't get soiled.)

Number of players: 2 to 8

Object: Students roll the dice and move the designated number of spaces. They must name a word beginning with the letter or letters shown. If they cannot name a word, they must move their counter back to its previous position. The first player to move across the finish line is the winner.

(This game is intended as a phonics review.)

Keep Away Words

Supplies needed: Dolch word cards, or flashcards derived from reading vocabulary.

Make flashcards using the text or materials to fit the student's needs. Use the Dolch list for any student deficient in basic sight vocabulary. The Dolch word cards may be used in class. Flashcards the student can keep and take home to show parents his progress are good motivators.

Number of players: 2

Object: Teacher or first player flashes a word. The other player says the word. For each word he knows, he gets to "keep" the card. He gets it "away" from the other player. Each word he doesn't know, the other player "keeps," and the student learns it for the next game.

(This game builds basic sight vocabulary, or vocabulary from the child's current reading materials.)

What's Missing?

Supplies needed: Five or six small objects, such as a ball, toy truck, block, etc. Different kinds of small toys may be used, or five or six wax fruits, such as are used to make a table decoration.

Number of players: 1 to entire class. (Any number).

Object: Teacher puts group of objects on table. The students look at the group, then cover their eyes. Teacher removes one or two objects from the group. Students then guess which objects were removed. This can be used as a team game, with the teacher keeping score. Team with most points wins. If played with one person, score may be kept, or just use this over as a guessing game.

(This game strengthens visual sequential memory.)

Merry Mix-up

Supplies needed: Five or six small objects, such as a ball, toy truck, block, etc. Different kinds of small toys may be used, or different geometric shapes. Wax fruits, such as are used in What's Missing, are excellent.

Number of players: 1 to entire class. (Any number).

Object: The teacher puts group of articles on the table, in an orderly line. Students look at the group, then cover their eyes. The teacher re-arranges the selection, switching one or two of the toys or fruits. Students guess which objects were switched. This can be used as a team game. The team with most points wins. If played with one person, score may be kept, or use this as a guessing game.

(This game is for visual sequential memory training.)

Where Am I?

Supplies needed: Key or small bell, or any object to make a light noise when dropped.

Number of players: Entire class or any number.

Object: The teacher darkens the room, and then stands at the back. She then rings the bell very lightly, or drops the key. Students must listen: then teacher calls on one who tells her the *exact* location of the sound. This can be used as a team game, or as an individual activity, with each child responding and keeping score. The teacher changes locations after each response, moving from place to place. Stress language use and strengthen laterality skills by having students designate back left, front right, next to the bookcase, etc.

(This game strengthens auditory memory skills.)

Funny Phrases

Supplies needed: Tagboard strips on which to write phrases. Primary sentence strip rolls (of heavy posterboard) are good, as you can cut these to any length.

Number of players: Entire class or any number.

Object: The player(s) take a Funny Phrase card and read it. Then he responds by making up a sentence of his own using the phrase. This can be used as an oral or a written activity. Also, it can be used to initiate story writing. Example: Use the phrase, "a tadpole and a tabby cat," or "a peck of pickled peppers for Peter."

(This activity reinforces phonics and vocabulary.)

Grocery Store

Supplies needed: None

Number of players: Entire class or any number.

Object: The first player starts the game by saying, "I went to the grocery store and bought . . .", then tells one item, such as butter. The next player repeats the sentence, giving the item mentioned previously and then adds his own. "I went to the grocery store and bought some butter and lettuce." Each player mentions previous items, then adds one. The winner is the player who can name all the items in order. (This game is similar to "Gossip" or "Telephone"). Teachers can make this a phonics game by having students give only items starting with the same sound, such as *p*eas, *p*epper, *p*otatoes, etc.)

(This game strengthens auditory memory skills.)

Silly Sentences

Supplies needed: Tagboard strips on which to write sentences. Primary sentence strip rolls are excellent.

Number of players: Entire class or any number.

Object: The player (or players) pick up a Silly Sentence card and read it. Then he responds by making up a story, including the sentence in it. This can be done orally or as a writing exercise. Example: "The boy had a bag of bubbles." or "The gang saw a gaggle of geese."

(This activity can reinforce phonics, be used as a vocabulary builder, and also will stimulate creative imagery.)

Word Ladders

Supplies needed: Ditto master, ditto paper. (Drill activity)

Number of players: Entire class or any number.

Object: Player or players takes the ditto sheet (see Figure 10-2) and attempts to "climb" the ladder, which is drawn thereon, by pronouncing all the words correctly. This can be adapted as a phonics exercise by omitting a key beginning sound, and having the student write it or say it.

(This is an excellent vocabulary builder, and can be used in conjunction with a basal reader, or the basic sight word list.)

Complete the Picture

Supplies needed: Ditto master, ditto paper. (Art activity)

Number of players: Entire class or any number.

Object: Player is given a ditto sheet (see Figure 10-3) with several lines, parts of circles, or an incomplete geometric figure. Then he takes crayons, and makes his own design or picture based on the figures given. I allow the student to turn the paper in any way he

CAN YOU CLIMB THE LADDERS?

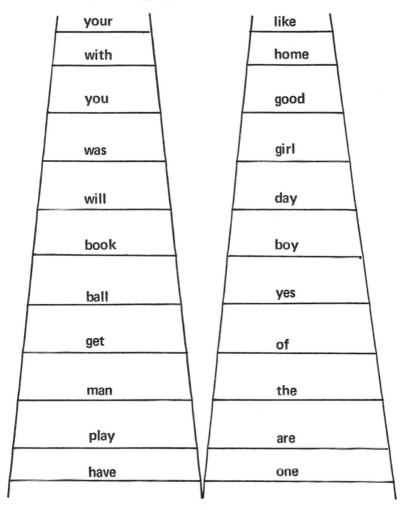

Figure 10-2

wishes (this changes the "attitude" of the incomplete symbols).

(This activity strengthens visual imagery, and creative critical thinking.)

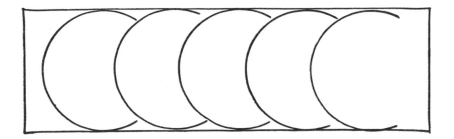

Figure 10-3

Dog and the Bone

Supplies needed: Student chair, chalkboard eraser.

Number of players: Entire class or any number.

Object: One person is it, and sits in the chair at the front of the classroom. He places the eraser (the "bone") under his chair and hides his eyes. The teacher or caller points out a student who "steals" the bone. The child quickly and quietly steals the eraser, hiding it in his desk. The class then chants:

> Doggie, doggie, guard your home.
> Somebody came and stole your bone!

The person who is "it" then has three guesses to find the "thief."

(This exercise helps strengthen motor control, for students trying to steal the bone, and auditory perception for the student who is "it.")

11

New Techniques and Individual
Teaching Methods – What We Can
Learn from Research and Development

Basic Research vs. Applied Research

B efore we begin to discuss changes in research, and there have been changes in the last 20 years, an explanation of terms is in order. "Basic research seeks broad generalizations to explain wide ranges of phenomenon."[1] Applied research on the other hand "seeks answers to narrower practical questions."[2] Basic research concerns itself with a wide range of theoretical questions, while applied research seeks answers to questions concerning "here and now."

Basic research seems to be that generated over a long period of time, thus providing more of a sociological view. It tends to

---

[1] *Encyclopedia of Educational Research*, Fourth Edition, Robert L. Ebel, ed. (American Educational Research Company, published by The MacMillan Company; 866 Third Ave. New York, N.Y. 10022, 1969), p. 1128.

[2] *Ibid.*

observe the problem, while offering less in the way of concrete solutions to the problem. Applied research is aimed at solving specific problems. Basic research tends toward the long view, that of working toward the ultimate good. Applied research on the other hand concentrates on more immediate concrete studies or techniques, usually carried out within the classroom. (With teachers and educators it seems to become a matter of priorities, with the most urgent and immediate problems attended to first.)

In researching problems in education, which is the better way? The conclusion as stated in the *Encyclopedia of Educational Research* is that research in education must be *both* basic and applied. "Without basic research, applied research becomes superficial and empty. Without applied research, basic research tends to become remote from educational problems."[3] This author would like to see applied research carried on over an extended period of time. From my own observations, I have noticed that studies carried on at the local level (school district or city-wide) tend to last only a few years at the most, and in some cases, hardly a year. I feel results from such a short program cannot be accurately measured.

Electronic Computer Effects on Research

In the past 15 or 20 years, electronic digital computers have been the single most important technological factor in changing educational research. Its greatest value has been in data analysis and in changing the technology of research. Where before, lengthy and varied calculations and recording of research data were expensive and time-consuming, the new computer banks which store and retrieve information have not only simplified research but have activated further research in education.

---

[3]*Encyclopedia of Educational Research,* Fourth Edition, Robert L. Ebel, ed. (American Educational Research Company, published by The MacMillan Company; 866 Third Ave. New York, N.Y., 10022, 1969), p. 1128.

Also, the nature of research technology has forced a change in attitude. New methods and ideas are needed to design a basic program of research that a computer can understand. In changing his language for this new research process, the researcher develops an insight into his own methods of research. The computer is thus forcing curriculum changes in schools, especially in graduate programs with graduate students acquiring a basic knowledge of computer language and matrix algebra, in addition to the usual natural language needed for advanced degrees.

In the future, we will see more and more computer-assisted instruction. Currently computers serve mostly as information processing and storage banks. (In my own school district, computer programming courses are now being offered in the high school. The end is not yet in sight!)

New Approaches in the Field of Reading

Over the past 20 years many teaching ideas and innovations have appeared in the field of reading. Among these are Phonetic Keys, the Phono-Visual method, the Initial Teaching Alphabet, Words in Color, the Unit Approach, the Linguistic Approach, Open Classrooms, and Individualized Learning, and last but not least, Learning Labs and Teaching Machines.

Phonetic Keys and the Phono-Visual method both stress extensive use of phonics, employing use of letter names and letter sounds. Proponents of these techniques suggest there is no need for the basic sight word list of 75 words until after the child knows the letter names and sounds, after which he applies this phonics knowledge to practice a meaningful sight vocabulary. Phono-Visual differs a bit from the Phonetic Keys in that it is taught as a separate subject (Organized Phonics) and then develops into the reading program. The authors stress that it is not a complete method by itself.

The Initial Teaching Alphabet also stresses sound, but uses an augmented Roman alphabet to assign a different character (printed symbol) to each of the 43 sounds of the English language. Sir James Pitman, who developed this method, states that it lessens visual disturbance as the child learns a different character for each sound. After the initial reading stages, the child gradually transfers to the traditional orthography. Proponents stress that the child gains confidence and mastery of the traditional spelling after six months to one year of I.T.A. training.

Under the Linguistic Approach, students are taught to see language patterns, and apply these in simple sentences. Lists of words are learned to enable the student to read meaningful sentences. Words in Color depends on charts and colored letters in initial or final position to give the child a visual key to pronunciation. For instance, the letter *f* at the beginning of *f*ield and the *gh* at the end of cou*gh* would be coded the same color, as they have the same consonant sound.

The Unit Approach, as suggested by Dilys Jones, lends itself more readily to middle grade skills development. With this method, the teacher and class decide on a basic theme or topic, which becomes the focus of class thinking and discussion. Emphasis in this method then centers on reading for meaning and to satisfy a need or interest. Independent research is stressed. This method correlates very closely with the Open Classroom techniques and Individualized Instruction. All of these place the burden of activities on the learner. Slower students will need much direction and guidance.

Perhaps the area of greatest concern and where most research has been concentrated is in the field of perceptual disabilities. More and better use of testing techniques and more materials to meet the needs of these students are being developed. Many colleges and universities are conducting long-range studies of students with learning disabilities.

Also, as stated earlier in the chapter, much more research is now going into evaluative instruments and testing techniques. Many new reading tests have been developed, and the older ones are being revised or redesigned. Most now include sections to test visual and auditory perception, which weren't incorporated into tests ten years ago. There is also more importance being attached to individualized type diagnostic tests.

My own feeling is that these individualized diagnostic tests can be of tremendous help to teachers who concentrate on individualized remedial reading instruction. The individual test situation affords the teacher an opportunity to judge not only how the student performs, test-wise, but also his attitude and behavior during the test. With the test observations in mind, an individual plan can be developed to best suit each student's needs.

The Changing and Broadening Forces in Remedial Reading

Since the era of Sputnik and President Johnson's "War on Poverty" there has been increased evidence of national interest in education as a whole, and reading and math in particular. There have been more government sponsored programs with federal funds being made available for research and development, and to implement programs in the classroom. As an example, since 1964 at least nine national research and development centers have been organized as part of the Cooperative Research Program of the United States Office of Education.

Out of all this and through national publicity via magazines and newspapers there has been a greater *public* awareness of and interest in our educational system. People are beginning to ask themselves, "Is our educational system doing what it is supposed to do?" Recently, a woman and her son brought suit against the school board of the city of San Francisco, California. The young man had graduated from high school, received his diploma, and yet couldn't read!

The *span* of general reading instruction is increasing. Heretofore, it was centered around elementary grades. Now, instruction is moving both up and down across a wide spectrum. There are many more preschool activities, such as "Project Head Start," and in California, the Early Childhood Education Act, which are designed to provide experiences and training so that children from all areas in the community are ensured a better chance at skills development. Children are encouraged to work and play in groups, and to learn to play with others. Parents are shown how to provide rich, meaningful experiences and many language activities to help their children learn to express themselves. California's Early Childhood Education Act stresses parent involvement. Funds are earmarked to train parents for work in the classrooms as teacher aides.

Because of this growing public interest, textbook publishers are taking a closer look at their own offerings. Books and supplemental materials are being written and revised to meet a growing clamor for newer, better materials. Many independent studies are being conducted to ascertain (1) what is needed, (2) what is wanted, and (3) what will meet individual differences.

There is greater interest focused on audiovisual equipment, teaching machines, and listening centers. Much of the new equipment is designed so that students can operate it themselves. Computer type equipment, "talking typewriters" and mechanical reading pacers are being developed. The use of "look-say" materials, where a card inserted in a slot activates tapes to play words so that students can repeat them, are becoming more and more popular for primary students. At junior high and high school levels, there is a growing use of reading pacers, learning labs, and auto-instructional devices.

Textbook manufacturers are also putting materials together in kit form, with reading levels covering a wide range, so that all abilities in a classroom might be bridged. In these, type is clearer, print is better, and the books come different sizes, to fit students' needs, not the classroom bookshelf. Many of these kits now contain "job cards" or related activities to stimulate independent research and critical thinking.

In the readers themselves, the focus is changing. No longer do we see Dick and Jane in a rural setting. Many of the newer texts are urban-oriented, showing photographs of city streets and urban children of many ethnic backgrounds. Emphasis is on functional everyday activities which take place in our changing technological society.

More remedial reading instruction is being offered at upper levels. Now reading specialists are using their skills to help junior high and high school instructors remediate within their own classrooms, while still teaching within their content areas. These same upper level teachers are more concerned with teaching their students how to read—not just presenting the material. They are willing and eager to at last have help in this long-neglected area.

Nowadays, many of our former jobs using manual labor have been automated. New jobs are programmed through computers, with everything done automatically. For example, in Crockett, California, there is a sugar processing plant where everything in one building is done by equipment, automatically. There isn't a person to be seen working on an assembly line. The building is empty—but the work is being done and the equipment is humming merrily away!

Prior to the last 20 years, many of the students graduating from high school would have gone to work in such a plant. They didn't go on to college. Because job techniques are changing, new types of training are now offered through the community colleges. Newer, sophisticated techniques are needed to keep up with our changing technology and our colleges are desperately trying to keep up with the growing need. Courses in computer programming, aircraft repair techniques, basic flying instruction, and real estate, to name a few, are the rule rather than the exception. All of these courses are currently being offered in our local community college, along with business and commercial courses and even leisure time activities, such as sailing, life-saving, and crafts such as cake decorating and foreign cookery, to meet not only academic needs, but also to provide skills for leisure time activities.

Because of this rapid change, more reading labs are being developed and used at community college and university levels. Many students are entering college without adequate reading and organizing skills and under new voluntary programs, these reading labs and their directors are provided to encourage students to improve and help themselves. Tutorial help, guidance, evaluation, and remediation are offered to these students.

To keep up with this growing cry for education, there is

more and greater involvement by local government and local industry. Courses are being offered which cost little or nothing to students involved, but provide them with on-the-job experience. For instance, recently in one of our local high schools, students were offered a course in "house building," which involved learning carpentry, architectural drafting, blueprint reading, electrical wiring, building codes, and so on. At the end of the course, the students had built a complete four room house which they promptly put up for sale. The proceeds were to be put back into the program to help finance another house!

In many instances industrial plants are sending their employees back to school and footing the bill. There are work-scholarship programs available, in which a student goes to college for one semester, then receives on-the-job training for one semester, providing practical application for skills and techniques learned in classes, and also providing funds enabling students to go to college who otherwise wouldn't have the opportunity.

Colleges and universities now offer five-year work-education programs similar to those previously described. Students who would otherwise find it difficult to attend college are encouraged to enroll in the program. Job placement is secured which fits with the student's major or academic interest, so that skills and education enhance and reinforce one another.

Many communities are also following this trend, and providing training in leisure time activities, and also participating in work-experience programs for high school students and young adults, where students work on the job and receive high school and college credit. Our high schools are also broadening their Outside Work Experience programs, so that students receive on-the-job training. Classes in our community are offered through local beauty colleges, automobile manufacturing plants, retail department stores (general merchandising), electronics, and in elementary schools (as teacher trainees), so that students can work in different fields and choose career goals, or even just "sample" different work experiences in order to make a career choice. All of these jobs need reading skills of some sort, and thus opportunities are provided for students to see, apply, and learn to appreciate how important reading is to earning a living.

12

Individual Evaluation and Setting Goals for Remedial Reading

This book has stressed helping the disabled reader, that is, the child who, for one reason or another, has difficulties in learning to read. (See Chapter 1.) Without help and remediation in school these potential dropouts become troublemakers, frustrated in their attempts to cope with life and their environment. Without adequate reading skills, they will probably join the ranks of the unemployed, or at best be able to hold only menial jobs. They deserve better than this, and it is our job to help these youngsters achieve success through a balanced remedial instructional program geared to their abilities.

The best way to balance your program for all students is to make it a four-step procedure:

(1) Diagnosis
(2) Remediation
(3) Maintenance
(4) Evaluation

These important steps should be common knowledge, and they have been discussed elsewhere, but I believe listing them step-by-step helps the reader to remember.

The first step is by testing and observation, to diagnose the exact nature of the students' disabilities.

Second, teach to these specific disabilities. Inherent in this is the thought that we remediate only *one* area at a time, so that students do not become confused or overwhelmed by too much material.

Third, you must not overlook maintenance and practice of skills already learned. Reinforcement is necessary so that students do not forget what they've already learned, as new skills are acquired.

Lastly, evaluation should be a constant, never-ending process. Test or observe continually, so that at any given moment you know exactly what skill is mastered, what is being taught, what needs *re*teaching and what to introduce next.

How to Set Up Instructional Program Guidelines

When setting up guidelines for your classroom program the basic objective is for every child to learn to read. Along with this we hope to instill in the child a *desire* to read, thus he not only can but *does* read, not only to learn, but for pleasure.

The child also needs to learn to be selective of his materials. He must evaluate and judge materials, reading and rejecting those ideas which are erroneous, or do not pertain to his situation. After evaluation, the child should be able to put what he has learned to use.

Start out by giving the student a choice of three or four books on his level pertaining to the subject he has chosen to investigate. In the primary grades, the responsibility for selection of a group of books rests on the teacher. At upper grades, responsibility can be a joint effort, with the teacher supplying a variety of books within the students' mastery and educational reading levels. Many of the new high interest-low vocabulary level series are designed for use with social studies areas, the study of ecology, or for such widely diverse area as great events in sports history or how a dune buggy is built. (A list of high interest-low vocabulary reading series is given at the end of this chapter.)

Children need to be taught to work together. This isn't a skill that comes automatically; they must be shown the reasons for working together, and they must be allowed a range of freedom (within their maturity level) to make their own mistakes and profit from them. They must also be given activities and tasks within their performance ability and geared to their interests and energy output.

There are several ways this can be done. One way is to use the buddy system. Let each child work with a friend. By pairing students of like ability, both work at a comfortable level, and their skills complement each other. You can use this not only as an initial learning tool, but also as reinforcement, simply by the nature of the assignments and your initial instructions when giving the lesson.

One activity which young children enjoy is play-making. By writing and producing their own play, they get many experiences in reading, role-playing, writing, etc., all of which help them learn to work together, and solve their problems successfully.

What the teacher makes available in the way of materials and supplies is also important. These should be geared to the children's performance level and interests as well as their attention span. Another important factor is the size of the group. Within a group you may have a wide range of ability. This must be kept in mind when helping children learn to work in groups.

I have mentioned earlier the use of high interest-low vocabulary reading series. Use the appropriate series as a starting point in teaching reference skills. Show students how to use the table of contents and the index in the book to locate information. From this point, start your library skills program, teaching the students to use the card catalog and the encyclopedias.

There are several filmstrips available illustrating library skills and demonstrating how to use them, if you feel uncomfortable in teaching these yourself. Take a large piece of plain tagboard and make a simulated card from the card catalog. Make it exactly like one from the card catalog. Show the title and author as is given on the original file card, and show the call number in its exact location (usually the left-hand corner) so that it corresponds exactly to the original. Then remove the file drawer from the large card catalog. Compare the original to the large (18" by 24") counterpart and, using both, go to the library shelf and locate the book. This concrete example helps the children to understand and *utilize* the card catalog to fullest advantage. I find this skill is assumed by too many teachers, each one thinking it has been taught in the past. In many cases this is true, but a good reference skills review will sharpen students' ability, and it also will teach the skill to a student who hasn't understood before, or who has not been in your school, and is unfamiliar with your library system. Remember, your slower students may have forgotten how to use the reference section, or were unable to learn. This gives them another chance at this very important skill.

The Easy Way Out

Why do teachers enter teaching? Is it to help students to learn? Or is it the easy way out? All too often teachers enter our profession with the idea of a safe, sane sinecure for life.

When this type of teacher finds a slow reader she (a) blames it on last year's teacher or (b) thinks his home environment might be to blame. She too, becomes a victim of "lock step" education, relying on "Round Robin Reading" and too many worksheets.

Obviously you, the reader, do not belong to this category. There *is* no easy way out. Teachers need to experiment and innovate to keep themselves fresh and their students motivated and interested. We as teachers need to do research, read books, magazines, pamphlets, and catalogs to find new techniques and materials; go to seminars and in-service meetings, and talk with school specialists (psychologist, nurses, etc.), and see what new information is available to help us in our field. It's often surprising how much help and information these people can provide.

Share your techniques, methods, and materials with your colleagues. Bread cast upon the waters comes back a thousand-fold. Recently I lent a teacher my teaching unit on Japan, complete with lesson plans, general outline, story books, costumes, and other realia. To my surprise a couple of days later I found materials pertaining to the unit I was constructing in my school mailbox. My colleague had *bought* the materials for me when she discovered them in a shop she frequented! Teaching is a give-and-take proposition. Share and the world shares with you.

So, back to my question. *Is* there any easy way out? The answer is, "NO." A dedicated teacher finds the work exhausting but exhilirating; tiring and tedious but also tantalizing. There's always something new to try next week!

Informal Reading Inventory

The first step in an informal reading inventory is to get to know your students. Take the time to talk with them. Observe their behavior on the playground and how they react to other students. Talk to last year's teacher. Use her prior knowledge to help assess the child's personality, needs, and interests, and then go to the cumulative records or the reading record cards. Check the information and skills recorded by previous years' teachers. The information and sometimes an insightful comment contained in these records can be very valuable. Every child is a diamond in the rough, and only the greatest skill can bring forth the beauty that is possible.

Third, check the reading *potential* of each student. What is he able to retain and understand?

Fourth, check the student's oral reading ability. Many methods have been suggested in earlier chapters. Two more are given in the next section.

Fifth, use a short checklist to record areas of strengths and weaknesses. There are many commercial checklists available, but most of these are fairly long. I would suggest making up a short checklist of your own, or keep a short anecdotal record for each child. Here again, I use the file card.

Finally, keep the sequence "spiraling" by continuous observation and evaluation. Use a systematic approach, and evaluate student progress as an on-going operation. Your program is only as effective as you make it, and the key to all this is the evaluation.

Oral Reading Check

In the preceding chapters I have given several methods to assess oral reading ability. Here are two final ones which may prove helpful: tape recording and self-selection.

Use tape recording as a pupil self-evaluating tool. Have the student select a page from a story he has read and rehearse it, making sure he understands all the vocabulary. Then have him read the selection aloud, recording on the tape. After this the student listens to the tape with your assistance, and thus he hears his own mistakes. Elicit from each student comments about his tape recording, so that he begins to find where he needs more practice in certain skills areas, or where he is making a mistake such as "backtracking" (reading a word several times before finishing the sentence.) When a student is aware of his own mistakes, then he can begin to correct them on his own and consciously work on the target areas. You will find this method very effective with upper elementary students.

For the self-selection method, pull books from your classroom library book shelf, and select books of varying degrees of difficulty, across all reading levels and all interests. Have the student choose one which he will enjoy and have him select a passage to read. As he reads, check for fluency, comprehension, and vocabulary mastery. This will help you find the child's instructional level.

Reading in the Content Areas

While much of primary instruction is centered around vocabulary building, stress in the upper grades should focus on other skills. The best way to assess reading ability is in the content areas. There are four purposes in checking through other curriculum areas: (1) vocabulary, (2) comprehension, (3) main idea, and (4) how to read and follow directions. Each of these is very important to the student's reading growth. Unless he understands what he reads and can utilize the information he is just "word calling." After learning basic word attack skills, he learns to read and pronounce the words correctly, and later on, learns to use expression. The next step is comprehension, understanding and applying what he reads.

The most important concept I have listed last—how to read and follow directions. However, I would judge it to be the most important concept of the four. The reason is that, to me, it is an on-going skill, one that every person uses throughout life. Therefore, the skill is taught as early as possible, and reinforced at every level. There are usually many cartoons, T.V. programs, and amusing articles published around Christmas showing unhappy fathers attempting to put toys together by following complicated directions given with the article. Believe me, these scenes are no joke! Many of these directions are poorly worded and lead to frustration on the part of those trying to follow them. I think part of this is due to ability to read directions. If you can't read directions, how can you write them for others to follow? So we have a two-fold problem: both writing directions and reading them. Since this is the case, there are two ways to help students learn to read and follow directions.

The first step is to help the child understand the directions for himself. I have the child read the directions, and then he must tell me in his own words what he must do. I use this in individual conferencing with students in reading, both for worksheet directions and for job cards on contracts, and we also practice it on our other subjects. When directions are given in the texts for English, spelling, or social studies, we put in our own words exactly what the problem is asking us to do. Again, this is an organizing, discrimination skill. Students must *understand* the directions, or they won't be able to put them into their own words, another way to check comprehension.

CAN YOU FOLLOW DIRECTIONS?

1. Put a red star on the left-hand corner of this paper.
2. Put a ring around the fifth word in this sentence.
3. Put a blue square on the right-hand corner of this paper.
4. Draw a line under the first, third, and fifth words in this sentence.
5. Put a green box around the red star on this paper.
6. Add two and two. Put your answer here. _____
7. Put a ring around the word "square" in problem 3.
8. Put a blue line under the fourth word in this sentence.
9. Put three orange lines under the blue square on this paper.
10. Subtract three from seven. Put your answer here. _____
11. Draw three circles on the end of this line.
12. Put a green triangle inside the blue square on this paper.
13. Put a fat black line under this sentence.
14. Put a yellow flower at the top of this page.
15. Sign your name at the bottom of this page.

Figure 12-1

Sample test in following directions. This is a pleasant way to reinforce lessons in following directions. This particular example is designed for use in grade two, second semester, or grade three, first semester. It can be adapted to any level by varying vocabulary and difficulty of the directions.

Students also need to learn to *give* directions. By organizing in sequence how to do things, they learn to think through a problem to a logical solution. It isn't easy for a second or third grader to tell anyone how to find his house to come over and play. Nor is it easy to describe how to fix pancakes. Yet it can, and should, be taught. In my class, one lesson I use regularly is "Tell how to get from our school to your house. Then draw me a picture map to show the way." Another lesson is to have students tell me their favorite food and how to prepare it. Then they draw a picture of how they do it, or of their finished product. True, many times they will leave out a step, but they begin to think in logical, sequential order—the first step in learning to give, and to follow, directions.

By the time most students reach the middle grades they have mastered basic sight vocabulary. Therefore, concentration on content vocabulary is the next step. Where there is new vocabulary presented in English, social studies, science, etc., the meanings must be explained, and terms mastered in context with the material presented. Terms such as atoms, molecular bonding, and inverse ratio are not self-explanatory. Be sure to take the time to *explain* new terms so that all students understand the material presented in other curriculum areas.

Once new specialized vocabulary is learned, students should have more training in how to read for understanding in different subjects. As stated earlier, there are key words and phrases to be learned in math problems to help students figure out what computational method is needed to set up and work the problem. The same is true in social studies and science. One method I have used in the past with middle and upper graders is most effective. Students read a paragraph from the text, then close their books. (You can also check reading speed by noting who finishes first.) I ask the question, "What is the single most important fact in that whole paragraph?" This helps students zero in on the main idea or topic sentence for the paragraph and is further practice in organizing and analyzing material, and in discarding extraneous information that is not pertinent (discrimination skill).

Another way to help students organize and find the main idea is to teach outlining skills. This again is a definite skill area and must be taught. You can expand the comprehension idea just mentioned in the preceding paragraph. Have students write down the most important fact in each paragraph, allotting one sentence per paragraph (sentence outline). Later, in class discussion, talk about finding supporting facts in the paragraphs, which expand information contained in the topic sentence of which provide insight into meaning. In this way, you can build skill and experience, so that you can teach *topic* outlining as a natural sequence.

Topic outlining is a very basic organizing skill. The earlier the concept can be taught, the better for a student's organizational skills development. If a student has an oral or written language deficit, he has a perceptual problem, and many times it can be spotted by the way he masters outlining technique, which is an organizational skill. I teach beginning outlining in second grade by use of the chalkboard. We list headings and sub-headings on experience charts and on the chalkboard for both social studies and science. Naturally, I do not expect my students to be able to put these in their own writing, but they see and become familiar with the form, and understand which parts are most important, thus, they are not entirely unfamiliar with it when they encounter it elsewhere.

Behavioral Objectives and How They Are Met

Today all over the country we hear the term "behavioral objectives." What is meant by this: Does it change our way of teaching? What is demanded in terms of goals for the teacher, student, and administration under these "new" guidelines? What *are* behavioral objectives? Why must they be written down, and why in terms of computer programming?

First of all, I think we need to clarify the difference between *goals* and *objectives*. "Goals are statements of broad, general outcomes of instruction and they do not state or convey meaning in a behavioral sense—they *do not tell* what the learner is to *do* at the end of instruction."[1] The behavioral objective, on the other hand, is much more specific. It states (1) what the learner is going to do, (2) what materials and methods will be available for the learner to use, (3) under what conditions the learner demonstrates his behavior, and (4) what evaluative techniques are to be used to measure this behavior?

When a long-term goal for the whole year is set it gives the teacher a focus, or target area, to aim for with the entire class. Out of this, we then describe in very specific terms what we expect from each student, or in some cases from a percentage of the students. Individualized learning and teaching strategies become part of the structure of behavioral objectives. Putting these objectives on paper may prove a little more difficult than stating them for whole class activities, but it can be done. For example: "The student will make the equivalent of one year's progress in phonics (in reading). Testing will be according to the Botel word list and the Macmillan grade level (end of book) test for _____ grade." (This objective uses two of the four criteria listed above. The other two, methods and materials, and the conditions would be contingent on the teacher's methods, etc.)

Utilizing behavioral objectives is a good way to check on progress, and to keep a record of what is attained. Second, for those teachers who have difficulty in record keeping, it provides the evaluative technique with which to measure pupil growth. Many teachers feel threatened by these cut-and-dried procedures, but our main concern should be for *pupil* progress, and target areas should be so stated that these purposes are at the top of the list. Behavioral objectives, as stated elsewhere, must be given in terms of the *learner*. His growth must be measured in terms of what *he* can accomplish and how much he can learn. The mark of a good teacher is how *well* the *learner* meets his behavioral objectives.

---

[1] Richard W. Burns, *New Approaches to Behavioral Objectives* (Dubuque, Iowa: Wm. C. Brown Company Publishers, 1972), p. 3.

FREMONT UNIFIED SCHOOL DISTRICT CERTIFICATED TEACHING PERSONNEL

PLANNING CONFERENCE FORM

Name _____   School or Office _____   Grade and Subject(s) _____   Date _____

Description of class composition (Circle any that apply):
Homogeneous   Heterogeneous   Self-contained   Departmentalized   Individualized   Other (Specify)

Expected Student Progress	Assessment Technique(s)	Instructional Method(s)	Unusual Circumstances	Additional Resources to be provided (Material or Administrative)
Who (the learner or learners)	Test Results, Performance attitude inventory.	Lectures	Class size	Special Aides
Will be able to do what (what behavior or accomplishment will take place)	Value Judgment	Discussions	Children with physical, emotional, or perceptual problems	Special Funds
	Product output -- quality or quantity	Video tape		Preparation time
		Tutors	Teacher illness	Administrative support
To what degree of proficiency (skill, accuracy, etc.)		Field trips	Other Existing Conditions	Provision for special or additional funds, equipment, materials, etc.
By when (quarter, semester, or during what time period)			Type of facility or teaching station	

Comments:

A teacher's greatest asset is that he is free to learn. Out of each teaching experience there develops a learning experience, and it is up to every teacher to profit from this.

How many of us have taught a lesson, only to see it go flat, half-way through? What do we do when this happens? In most cases, the majority of teachers have profited from the experience and have developed what one of my college professors called a "bag of tricks" to fall back on. We quickly change directions or goals, to try to reach our students.

It is my hope that this book has offered suggestions and teaching techniques in quantity so that you, the reader, have added to your bag of tricks, and that it enables you to reach the goals you set for your individualized remedial reading program.

Figure 12-2

Page one of a three-page planning conference form to be used in setting up behavioral objectives. Reprinted by special permission, Fremont Unified School District, Fremont, California 94538.

Selected List of

HIGH INTEREST-LOW VOCABULARY READING SERIES

The materials listed herein are not the "be-all and end-all" of High Interest-Low Vocabulary series available, but are only a *sampling* of those found in one school district's Intructional Materials Center. The author suggests that these are only a small portion of the materials available; in fact, just the tip of the iceberg. Use these as a beginning and from this "jumping off point" find the materials that suit your needs and the needs of your students.

1. *Time Machine Series,* Gene Darby and Richard Hornaday (authors.) Field Educational Publications, Inc., San Francisco, 1968. Controlled vocabulary, pre-primer through 2.5, based on *Spache Readability Formula* and *Dale List of 769 Easy Words.* Records to go with each of the eight books in the series. To be used in small groups or individually. On the use of the records, the authors state, "Letting a child hear a story as he reads it from the book enables him to familiarize the vocabulary and to recall words he may momentarily have forgotten." (p. 3, Teachers Manual.)

2. *Button Family Adventures,* Edith S. McCall, Benefic Press, Chicago, 1964. Pre-primer to third grade level. 12 books. Vocabulary based on L.L. Krantz, *The Author's Word List for the Primary Grades,* and *The Teacher's Word Book of 30,000 Words* by Edward Lee Thorndike and Irving Lorge. Suggested as supplemental to basal readers; as transitional materials from textbook to free reading. Suggested for use through fourth grade.

3. *Cowboy Sam Series,* Edna Walker Chandler, Benefic Press, Chicago, 1961. Pre-primer to grade three level. 15 books, controlled vocabulary suggested, but no mention of which word list is used as basis for control. Suggested as supplemental to basic readers for grades one to three, remedial for grades, four, five, and up.

4. *The Jim Forest Readers,* John Rambeau, Harr Wagner Publishing Company, San Francisco, 1959, primer to third grade, 6 books. Controlled vocabulary based on *Dale List of 769 Easy Words* and Gates wordlist, *A Reading Vocabulary for Primary Grades.* Ideally suited for retarded readers in late primary or middle grades (adventures based on the life of a forest ranger).

5. *Dan Frontier Series,* William Hurley, Benefic Press, Chicago, 1964. Eleven books, pre-primer to grade four. Controlled vocabulary, based on L.L. Krantz and Thorndike-Lorge (see no. 2). Suggested as after-basic supplementary reading and as reinforcement and skill builder.

6. *Sailor Jack Series,* Susan and Jack Wassermann, Benefic Press, Chicago, 1962. Ten books, pre-primer to grade three level. Editor suggests these books be used to stimulate critical thinking (based on research of Dr. Louis E. Raths, Professor of Education, New York University). Controlled vocabulary suggested, but basis not given.

7. *Dolch First Reading Books,* Edward W. Dolch and Marguerite P. Dolch, Garrard Publishing Co., Champagne, Ill., 1958. Over 15 books, levels pre-primer through 2^2. Based on Dolch Basic Sight Word List. Designed to Strengthen vocabulary and stimulate independent reading for slow learners. (While these books are older, they are still very good, and are interesting reading.)

8. *American Adventure Series,* Albert Betts, ed., Harper and Row Publishers, Inc., Pleasanton, Ca. Twenty-one books, Levels A1 to E4 (second through sixth). Mostly biographies of famous people. Suggested teacher guide *Handbook on*

Corrective Reading to be used in correlation with series. Controlled vocabulary based on Dr. Betts' studies of basic reader vocabularies. There is a wordlist to be mastered *before* the student reads each text (given in the front of the teachers' manuals.)

9. *Interesting Reading Series,* Morton Botel, ed. Follett Publishing Company, Chicago, 1968. Eleven books, 2^2 to 3^2. Based on great events in history, sports—a diversity of topics to stimulate interest. Several books adaptable to social studies reinforcement, fifth and sixth grades. Controlled vocabulary based on *Botel Reading Inventory.*

10. *Morgan Bay Mysteries,* John and Nancy Rambeau, Harr Wagner Publishing Company, San Francisco, 1965. Eight books in series, level 2.3 to 4.0. Primarily for use from fourth to ninth grade, as high interest—low vocabulary, and as supplemental reading, second through fourth grade.

11. *World of Adventure Series,* Henry Bammann and Robert Whitehead, Benefic Press, Chicago, 1965. Eight books, level 2.5 to 6.0 Based on L.L. Krantz and Thorndike-Lorge Word Lists (see no. 2). Suggested for pupils at intermediate and junior high who are encountering reading difficulties and are reading below grade level. Also suggested for supplemental in primary grades for students reading on grade level.

12. *Deep Sea Adventure Series,* James C. Coleman, et al., Harr Wagner Publishing Co., San Francisco, 1962. Designed to raise reading skills to fourth grade level. Eight books in series, to be used in small groups or individually.

13. *Wildlife Adventure Series,* William S. Briscoe and John A. Hockett, Harr Wagner Publishing Co., San Francisco, 1966. Eight books, under achievers from grade four on. Suggested for use after *Deep Sea Adventures* to take advantage of large overlapping vocabulary. Reading level range 4.1 to 5.5 Controlled vocabulary based on word lists of the primary grades.

14. *Learning to Read While Reading To Learn Series,* Joe Stanchfield, et al. Century Communications, San Francisco, 1969. Eighteen books, suggested for upper elementary and junior high. (Most books in the series are at or near fourth grade reading level, interest level through junior high school.)

15. *Checkered Flag Series,* Henry A. Bammann and Robert J. Whitehead, Field Educational Publications, Inc., San Francisco, 1968. Five books, suggested for use in junior and senior high school, and also in upper elementary. Suggested basic vocabulary, but no source given.

16. *Reading Incentive Series,* Ed and Ruth Radlauer, Bowman, Glendale, Ca. 91201, 1971. Authors state they purposely did not assign a grade level to the books, suggesting that teachers use them in the classroom to find out. I would suggest upper elementary, junior high, and high school. However, I have had second grade boys check these out and thoroughly enjoy them, particularly the drag racing and dune buggy books. Records, tapes, and film strips for use also available.

BIBLIOGRAPHY

Alternative Schools: Pioneering Districts Create Options for Students. Arlington, Va: National Schools Public Relations Association, 1972.

Armstrong, Dr. Robert J., et al, editors. *A Systematic Approach to Developing and Writing Behavioral Objectives.* Tucson, Ariz: Educational Innovators Press, Inc., 1968.

Artuso, Alfred et al. *Individualized Reading Skills Improvement.* Denver: Love Publishing Co., 1971.

Botel, Morton. *Botel Predicting Readability Levels.* Chicago: Follett Publishing Company, 1962.

Bremer, Anne and John Bremer. *Open Education, A Beginning.* New York: Holt, Rinehart and Winston, 1972.

Burns, Richard W. *New Approaches to Behavioral Objectives.* Dubuque, Iowa: Wm. C. Brown Company, Publishers, 1972.

Carter, Darrell B., ed. *Interdisciplinary Approaches to Learning Disorders.* Philadelphia: Chilton Book Co., 1970.

Chall, Jeanne. *Learning to Read: the great debate.* New York: McGraw-Hill, 1967.

Cordts, Anna D. *Phonics for the Reading Teacher.* New York: Holt, Rinehart and Winston, 1965.

Dechant, Emerald. *Diagnosis and Remediation of Reading Disability.* West Nyack, N.Y.: Parker Publishing Company, Inc., 1968.

Education, U.S.A. *Individualization in Schools.* Washington, D.C.: National School Public Relations Association, n.d.

Encyclopedia of Educational Research, Fourth Edition. Robert L. Ebel, ed. New York: The MacMillan Company, 1969.

Esbenson, Thorwald. *Working With Individualized Instruction.* Belmont, Ca: Fearon Publishers, 1968.

Featherstone, W.B. *Teaching the Slow Learner.* New York: Teachers' College, Columbia University, 1951.

Frostig, Marianne and David Horne. *The Frostig Program for the Development of Visual Perception* (Teacher's Guide). Chicago: Follett Publishing Co., 1964.

Gans, Roma. *Fact and Fiction about Phonics.* New York: Bobbs-Merrill Co., 1964.

Glasser, Joyce Fern. *The Elementary School Learning Center for Independent Study.* West Nyack, N.Y.: Parker Publishing Co., 1971.

Goslin, David A. *Teachers and Testing.* New York: Russel Sage Foundation, 1967.

Heilman, Arthur W. *Teaching Reading.* Columbus, Ohio: Charles E. Merrill Books, 1961.

Johnson, G. Orville. *Education for the Slow Learners.* Englewood Cliffs, N.J.: Prentice-Hall, Inc., 1963.

Kirk, Samuel A. and Winifred D. Kirk. *Psycholinguistic Learning Disabilities: Diagnosis and Remediation.* Urbana, Ill: University of Illinois Press, 1972.

Learning Centers: Children on Their Own, Virginia Rapport, ed. Washington, D.C.: Association for Childhood Education International, 1970.

Mazurkiewicz, Albert J., ed. *New Perspectives in Reading Instruction.* New York: Pitman Publishing Corporation, 1964.

Mehrens, William A. and Irvin J. Lehmann. *Standardized Tests in Education.* New York: Holt, Rinehart and Winston, 1969.

Money, John. *The Disabled Reader.* Baltimore: Johns Hopkins Press, 1966.

The Open Classroom, Informal Education in America (An Occasional Paper). Dayton, O: Institute for Development of Educational Activities, Inc. (I.D.E.A.), 1972.

The Open Plan School (An Occasional Paper). Dayton O: Educational Facilities Laboratories, Inc. and I.D.E.A., 1973.

Raymond, Dorothy. *Individualizing Reading in the Elementary School.* West Nyack, N.Y.: Parker Publishing Co., 1973.

Robinson, H. Allen and Ellen Lamar Thomas, eds. *Fusing Reading Skills and Content.* Newark, Del: International Reading Association Yearbook, 1970.

Roswell, Florence and Gladys Natchez. *Reading Disability.* New York: Basic Books, Inc., 1964.

Silberman, Melvin, et al. *The Psychology of Open Teaching and Learning, An Inquiry Approach.* Boston: Little, Brown and Co., 1972.

Smith, Nila Banton. *Reading Instruction for Today's Children.* Englewood Cliffs, N.J.: Prentice-Hall, Inc., 1963.

Smith, Robert M., ed. *Teacher Diagnosis of Educational Difficulties.* Columbus, O.: Charles E. Merrill Publishing Co., 1969.

Staiger, Ralph and David A. Sohn, eds. *New Directions in Reading.* New York: Bantam Books, 1967.

Teachey, William G. and Joseph B. Carter. *Learning Laboratories.* Englewood Cliffs, N.J.: Educational Technology Publications, 1971.

Valett, Robert E. *Modifying Children's Behavior.* Belmont, Ca.: Fearon Publishers, 1969.

—————, *Programming Learning Disabilities.* Belmont, Ca: Fearon Publishers, 1969.

—————, *The Remediation of Learning Disabilities.* Belmont, Ca: Fearon Publishers, 1967.

Van Witsen, Betty. *Perceptual Training Activities Handbook.* New York: Teachers College, Columbia University, 1967.

Veatch, Jeannette. *Individualizing Your Reading Program.* New York: G.P. Putnam's Sons, Van Ness Press, 1959.

Weisgerber, Robert A. *Perspectives in Individual Learning.* Ithaca, Ill.: F.E. Peacock Publishers, 1971.

Index